PERSIAN AND OTHER ORIENTAL CARPETS
for Today

To my wife Ann with love and devotion

PERSIAN AND OTHER ORIENTAL CARPETS
for Today

Nicolas Fokker

London   George Allen & Unwin Ltd
Ruskin House   Museum Street

Contents

First published in 1973. Second revised edition 1975. Second impression 1976
Reprinted 1976

© 1973 Interbook Publishing AB
Produced by Interbook Publishing AB
Box 3159 S-103 63 Stockholm
English translation by Keith Bradfield
Drawings by Arthur Hardie
Printed in Great Britain by
Hazell Watson and Viney Ltd
ISBN 0-04-746005-9

An Oriental Craft

Before acquiring an oriental carpet for your home, you will be wise to acquire at least an elementary knowledge of Persian carpets. Without its implying any suspicion of the seller, you should be able to judge for yourself why the one carpet is dearer than the other, when both are of the same type and practically identical size. Informative labelling is unknown in the trade, and there are no recommended prices; nor can there be, because we are concerned with a work of oriental craftsmanship, not with mass-produced wares of identical pattern, quality and size. It is hardly surprising that the most desirable carpets should also be the most expensive: as a rule, they are of higher quality.

If you already own a carpet you like, you still will not have the proper relationship with it until you have discovered the meaning of its ornamentation and colors, the origin of its pattern. There is much to discover, on the tiniest piece of your carpet. The world over, illiterate people have expressed their faith, their history, their legends, their superstitions, their magic and visions in images, colors and symbols. Some of which may well have found their way into your carpet. Asia is steeped in the mystery of many religions. If it has never before occurred to you that dead things can speak, turn to the archeologists or zoologists and find out what tales can be told by a painted shard of earthenware or fragment of bone!

The language of Persian carpets is full of fantasy. Studying the pattern of a carpet more closely, you may discover several details that you seem to have encountered in other contexts. A knot of eternity you saw once on a Chinese vase, a meander from an Etruscan mural or Greek amphora. You may be surprised to find Ionic columns supporting the arch on a prayer carpet, and suspended from the arch a Byzantine lamp. A water jug of the kind women still bear on their heads in Mesopotamia can recall the Bible illustrations of Gustave Doré. On another carpet, we may see a winged lion with the bearded head of a man: its predecessors still watch faitfully over the ruins of Assur and Niniveh. A lotus flower carries our thoughts to the tombs of the Pharaohs, while human figures with strange animal heads relate to the mysticism of India.

It is strange what deep traces have been left by the numerous military campaigns of world history. Countless carpets woven by illiterates in desolate Persian villages bear witness to an inheritance from Cyrus, Darius, Alexander the Great and the archers of Chosrau Parvez, of the Arab hordes of the first Caliphs, or the horsemen of Genghis Khan and Tamerlane. As the waves of history washed over Asia, Persia was overlaid with the stratified impressions of the culture and art of peoples that came and vanished. With exquisite taste, Persian artists sifted from this sediment the loveliest symbolic and decorative motifs, and incorporated them with their own. All this, which fused in time into a heterogeneous Persian art, has left its mark on every carpet, great or small, cheap or expensive. What you are acquiring is thus a work of craftsmanship, which has no identical fellow, and which, beyond its purely commercial value, offers something very difficult to define.

There are no standard rules that can be applied in the choice between different Persian carpets, but the following chapters offer a variety of facts, tips and suggestions that may help you find the right carpet at the right price.

The History of the Persian Carpet

The history of oriental carpets remained unknown until the mid 19th century. Only then did the historians of art concern themselves with carpets. Carpet-weaving began to be regarded as a branch of Islamic art.

It was difficult to get started. The museums had no collections to show. Scholars were forced to visit castles and palaces, copy patterns, and inquire about the origins of the carpets. In most places, records had been kept of when and how these carpets had come into the family's possession. Italian, Flemish and German Renaissance and Baroque painters often portrayed oriental carpets in their pictures, where they were depicted as covering floors or tables. Since the dates of these artists were known, it was possible roughly to determine the age of certain carpets. Antique oriental brocades, the decorated ceramic tiles on the walls of mosques, and the engravings on metal artifacts from different eras provided a comparative material, and helped in the search for further knowledge. Mistakes as regards date or place of manufacture were inevitable but were gradually corrected as new and more reliable facts emerged. Gradually, the districts in which the majority of patterns occurred were successfully charted. Great progress was made in the course of a few decades. However, all attempts to follow the trail further back than the 15th century were defeated. The occasional carpet or fragment seemed to be of earlier date — the famous Konya carpet in Turkey, for instance, is believed to have been made in the 12th century — but no fully convincing evidence could be found.

The age and origin of the carpet

The main object of research was to establish when and where carpets first began to be manufactured. From passages in the Bible and classical literature, the conclusion was drawn that the oriental art of carpet-making was known and applied long before the birth of Christ.

Homer speaks of a "couch covered with a purple carpet".

Xenophon waged war against the Persians in 401 B.C. He reports that "the Persians customarily lie on soft carpets". On another occasion, he mentions a carpet as being worth 10 minas = 13.6 lb silver.

The only conclusion to be drawn from these passages is that the cult of the bed stems from the Orient; however, they say nothing as to whether these carpets had a *pile* or were woven with some other technique.

Mediaeval Europeans must surely have come into contact with oriental carpets during the Crusades. No record, however, exists to this effect. In Europe, at that time, it was mainly the monks who could write, and if any manuscripts on carpets still exist they are hidden in the often inaccessible libraries of the monasteries.

Probably the oldest known European manuscript to mention carpets is dated to about 1150. A rabbi by the name of Petachja from Regensburg undertook an adventurous journey to visit those of the same faith in New Niniveh and Baghdad, then at the height of their glory. He mentions, in his account of the journey, a visit to Halevy, Prince of the Jews, a descendant of King David, who "lives in a grand house, furnished with rich carpets". The wording seems to suggest that the house was furnished mainly with expensive carpets — a custom that still has its grip on the Oriental. It is so deeply rooted that the well-off even today cover their arm-chairs and sofas with carpets.

Not until the 14th century are carpets described in any more detail, in a couple of Arabian travel letters. These, however, are of no importance from the standpoint of research. The carpets, demonstrably from the 15th and 16th centuries, to be found in the possession of various museums are of such high standard that we must assume them to have been preceded by an extremely long period of development. The question is — how long?

We do not know where or when people first began to spin yarn and weave cloth, in Goethe's words "the oldest and most glorious art, that which truly began to separate man from the animals".

Equally little is known of the genesis of carpets. Perhaps, in the beginning, it was from a playful whim: someone had the idea of knotting a few tufts of wool into a woven fabric, to resemble a sheepskin. If so, the idea proved a splendid discovery. A sheepskin, when exposed to moisture and sunshine, became stiff and heavy as a plank. The new material was at least as warm, but infinitely lighter and much softer. This primitive artifact became the prototype of what we now call a hooked rug. It was a great step forward even to use such "carpets" instead of the odorous flayed skins with which the caveman furnished his home. After this phase of development, however, infinite years must have passed before another man discovered the short-cut, namely *to knot in the pile while the cloth was being woven*. With this, the oriental carpet had been invented. The technique required no perfection: even today, carpets are knotted by the same method as was used in the world's first oriental carpet.

The next step was the decoration.

The first pattern probably consisted of stripes or idiographs. These were later followed by religious or magical symbols. More imaginative patterns, and the discovery that a shorter, more evenly cut pile, set the pattern off more effectively, gave a new, more artistic touch to the carpet. From having been a simple utility object, it was raised to the level of art. The spinning of the yarn more evenly, the improvement of dyeing techniques and variations in pattern were mere refinements.

For many, many ages to come, the pattern was geometrical — drawn in straight lines. The curved pattern requires a carefully drawn cartoon on squared paper, and is a fairly late development in the carpet's history. The nomad carpets, and those made in the numerous small villages, almost always have a geometrical pattern.

Asia gave birth to the first great civilizations in human history. The people of Asia were familiar with bronze 2,000 years before the "Europeans", who were still living in caves or pile-dwellings and manufacturing their tools and weapons from stone. All scholars unreservedly agree that the carpet comes from Asia. But from what part of that enormous continent?

Turkestan has had the most champions, followed in quick succession by Persia, Mongolia and Caucasia. Mesopotamia has not been suggested owing to its fairly large barren areas, although great climatic changes are known to have occurred there in the last millennia. But who has dared think so far back in time in relation to carpets?

It seemed only logical that the vast pasturelands of Turkestan, with their giant herds of sheep and goats which gave an excess of wool, should have given birth to the art of carpet-making. But this was only an hypothesis. The idea of making a carpet hardly needed millions of sheep for its generation, one would have been more than enough. Probably, it was somehow a question of chance — or intelligence.

The original inhabitants of the Euphrates' delta, the Sumerians, **The Sumerians** were also a highly developed people. Only a few generations ago, nothing was known of their civilization. It was only guessed or deducted that they ever existed. The Sumerians, whose origins are lost in obscurity, are regarded as the inventors of cuneic writing. They composed religious poems, instituted laws and recorded their legends on the Creation. Their account of the Flood was taken over by the Babylonians and Hebrews. And it was confirmed in the late 20's by excavations at Ur of the Chaldees, birthplace of the patriarch Abraham, where silt deposits up to four metres thick were found between two plans of settlements some 5,000 years old. The archeologists were confounded by the well-preserved artifacts revealed: a helmet of pure gold, goblets of beaten gold, hair-pieces. Filigree work on daggers, vessels, statuettes, reliefs in metal, stone or clay, all of exquisite form and ornamentation, superbly executed. There was no doubt that they were on the trail of a highly advanced civilization.

Further testimony to the skill and ingenuity of Sumerian artists is borne by numerous finds of mosaic work, incorporating gold, silver, lapis lazuli, mother-of-pearl, shells, and various stones and woods.

From the standpoint of the historian of carpets, these mosaics are the most interesting of all. Because what is a carpet but a mosaic executed in yarn of different colors rather than colored stones, metal or wood? Conceivably, we have here the source of inspiration from which the art of carpet-weaving arose.

But whether or not it was the Sumerians who first thought of the idea of imitating mosaics with the help of yarn, we cannot say. The clay tablets found have as little to say of carpets as of the origin of mosaics. Wool quickly moulds away in the earth, not the smallest fragment has been found that could be traced to a carpet. A large number of special conditions are required for certain objects to be preserved for any length of time under the earth.

The carpet of Pazyryk and the obelisk of Salmanassar

Thanks precisely to such special conditions, a carpet was found in a 2,500 year old tomb — a carpet in the strict sense of the word, knotted, and with a pile!

In the years 1947—49, Russian archeologists working in the Pazyryk Valley in Altai in Southern Siberia excavated the tomb of a Scythian chieftan; by a fortunate accident, this had been filled with water and frozen into a giant block of ice. The ice had preserved everything in the tomb; the corpse, horses, clothing, saddles — and a carpet.

The Pazyryk carpet is almost square — 6 ft 7 in × 6 ft — and, considering the circumstances, well preserved. Its quality is surprisingly high, 232 knots per square inch, more densely knotted than most of the carpets now sold in the trade. It gives a pleasant, warm impression with rust and brown-black mottling, like that of the painted figures in the Altamira cave, against the natural, light wool.

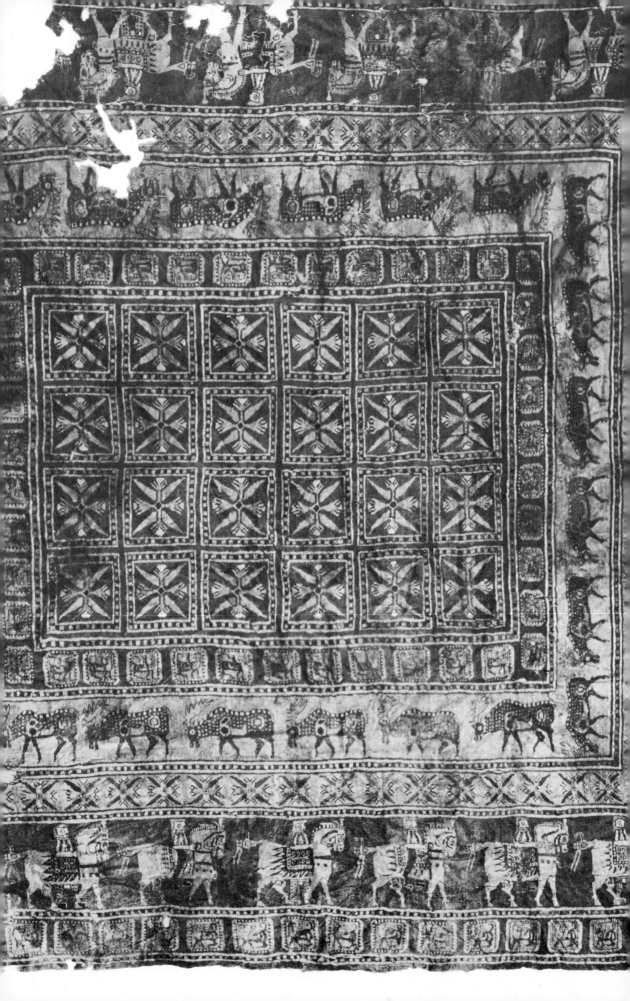

The composition of the pattern is remarkable. In the inner, main border, a herd of reindeer stalk in procession round the carpet; in the outer border, Persian horsemen are filing past in the opposite direction. The impression is of an exotic exhibition of dressage by riders dressed up as warriors from the great days of the Persian Empire. Further life and content are lent to the composition by the fact that occasional riders have dismounted, and are leading their horses on foot.

The 20 squares of the central field all carry the same ornamentation: a vertical bar, slit into a V at both ends, with broken diagonals in the middle. The latter taper off towards the mid-point, like an exclamation mark. The pattern is supplemented by four points symbolizing the points of the compass. Similar ornamentation has been found on Assyrian reliefs and Egyptian papyri.

The overall impression is overwhelming. One is forced to the conclusion that this is a Persian carpet, and that such an advanced piece of craftsmanship must have been preceded by a very long period of development. The same reflection, then, on contemplating a carpet 2,500 years old as occurred to the scholars seeing carpets made in the 16th century A.D.

We have thus been given a slight hint of where it all began. The question that remains is when.

The Assyrian ruler Salmanassar III (c. 850 B.C.) caused an obelisk to be raised in his honor, in which, following royal tradition, he ordered that his victorious exploits should be hewn in cuneic text and illustrative pictures. This obelisk depicts, among other things, the envoys of subjected neighbours bearing tributes. Two men from neighbouring Elam in southern Persia are carrying two rolled-up carpets as a tribute from their king. These carpets must have been rated very highly if two pieces, probably 5 ft × 3 ft 3 in, sufficed as tributes.

Here, the trail comes to an end.

Excavations in Susa, the capital of Elam, have shown that the people there were also artistically very gifted, and that the Sumerian and Elamite cultures influenced each other. Since the art of carpet-weaving in the past millennia has nowhere to our knowledge reached such heights as in Persia, it would be heartening if future finds provided evidence that the world's first carpet had been woven on Persian soil.

The importance of Islam for carpet-making

If carpets, in 850 B.C., were exclusive gifts exchanged between kings, they became, in as many years A.D., the property of ordinary men throughout much of the Near East and Central Asia. This service was rendered by Islam, the new religion forced upon the continent. Since its ritual demanded that the daily five prayers should

The Pazyryk carpet. The Hermitage Museum, Leningrad.

be recited in the kneeling position and on a clean surface, there rapidly arose among the newly converted a need for millions and millions of small prayer carpets.

The Arabian nomad peoples were unaware of the existence of carpets until they arrived in Persia as conquerors. The Koran does not require that prayers should be said on a carpet, it says nothing about the subject. And the "Commentaries to the Koran" simply state that prayers should be said kneeling on something *clean,* and sufficiently heavy for the wind not to blow it away. What could be more simple than a carpet, heavy enough to lie still when the wind was blowing, light enough to carry when travelling, and something that only had to be shaken to be clean? This latter was particularly important in those unfortunate countries where people digging for water found only oil!

Our first referense to the existence of prayer carpets is from an early 8th century Persian source. Hussein, Mohammed's nephew, and the foremost saint of the Shiite Persians, was martyred at Karbela on 2 August 680. Since that time the earth around his grave has been regarded as holy. From this earth are made small pats called "myhur", against which the faithful press their foreheads when reciting their prayers. The custom is said to stem from the Imam Mohammed Bakir, Hussein's grandson, who for 40 years bewept the death of the martyr, and "to be able to think of his fate more intensively, was accustomed to strew a few grains of sand from his grave on the prayer".

The advance of Islam was marked by new mosques, built by vainglorious Shahs, Emirs, Grand Moguls and Khans to bear their names. The floors were covered with splendid, extra large showpiece carpets, replenished over the centuries by generous donations.

To an increasing extent, people's homes were also decorated with carpets, whether the dwelling in question was a palace, a hovel or a tent. Every family acquired its loom, the women and children soon learnt the art of weaving. The small prayer rugs paved the way for larger carpets; the floors were covered and doors replaced by carpets, which now also decorated the previously bare walls.

The whole thing avalanched. Carpets were manufactured in a never-failing torrent. Girls wanted to demonstrate their skill and affection for their future husbands, by conferring upon them attractively woven carpets and saddle-cloths. Even simple, practical utility items like sacks, camel and donkey bags, previously made of goatskin, began now to be woven, knotted and decorated with artistic embroidery. The makers' skill and fantasy were trained up to undreamed-of heights.

The carpets in the mosques were sacral, they were regarded as a sort of religious "property". As a result, graves too began to be decorated with carpets. In that carpets in the home were unconsciously associated with those in the mosques, the former too were regarded with reverence. Carpets became a sort of family "best furniture", appreciated for their value and as status symbols.

The manufacture of carpets must have gone in waves, with artistic and quantitative peaks followed by periods of deep decadence. Persia suffered wars and occupations, was plundered by the Assassins, the Seljuk Turks of Genghis Khan and Tamerlane, and by the Ottomans. There was no time over for the peaceful concentration required to produce great carpets, nor was there any point in making them.

The oriental carpet in Europe

Europe had to wait a long time for its Persian carpets. No one, in fact, missed them. The continent was tired and decimated by the wars, plagues and famines that had followed the great migrations and Crusades. The dark blinds of the Middle Ages had been carefully drawn, so that no light could seep in from the outside. Only Venice and Genoa, the great powers of the 14th century, had connections with the Orient. And to these cities came the first carpets, which were in fact of Turkish origin. The need had forced the Turks to learn to weave their own prayer carpets, simple works of handicraft indeed by comparison with their perfected Persian models. Like the Sunnites, i.e. orthodox Mohammedans, the Turks depicted neither people, animals nor even flowers on their carpets. In spite of their coarse pattern and simple quality, these carpets were a great success, particularly in Venice, where palace floors, balconies, tables, even the gondolas of the aristocracy were covered with them, as we can see from the works of late Mediaeval painters and Renaissance artists.

Persian carpets did not reach Europe until the 17th century. The Netherlands and Portugal were then the great sea-powers, enjoying much wider contacts with the Orient than ever Venice or Genoa. Only naturally, the first Persian carpets were imported to these countries.

The time coincided with the classical age of the Persian carpet. Persia was ruled by the Safavid sun-king Shah Abbas the Great, a generous patron of architecture and art. He left Kazvin, with its exposed camp, and instead built up Isfahan as the new capital. Its stately palaces and mosques had to be furnished with worthy carpets, and he called upon Persia's most famous miniature painters and calligraphers to compose patterns for them, the most skilled weavers to execute them. Carpets of a beauty never previously achieved were conjured forth on the looms in the Shah's workshops. The material ranged from the fairest woollen yarn to the finest silk, silver and gold threads. This hum of activity, and the affluence of the period, stimulated carpet-weavers in other cities; as a result, the most exclusive carpets ever produced were created in 16th century Persia.

As in pre-Islamic time, the finest of them went to the Shah and the court nobles. Ordinary people had no chance of acquiring such treasures. Even in Europe, the few Persian carpets to arrive were destined for royal courts or princely houses. Sometimes, the Shah envoys to different European courts took carpets with them as gifts. This, for instance, was the case with the famous hunting carpet that belongs to the Swedish royal house, and that previously owned by the Habsburgs, now the pearl of the Wiener Handelsmuseum's collection. Both are of silk and threads of noble metal, and are the finest to be seen in any western collection.

Shortly after the death of Abbas the Great, diplomatic relations with Europe were broken. Persian carpets, previously so rare, were seen no more. And once the Afghans had invaded part of Persia in the 18th century, all organized carpet-weaving in Persia stopped.

So few people in Europe owned Persian carpets, that the latter were soon forgotten. Instead, merchants from Constantinople began to reintroduce Turkish carpets on the European market. These carpets, now regarded as classical — Ushak, Ghiordes, Siebenburgener, Ladik, Kula etc. — were of smaller format, c. 4 × 6 ft, and their price made them available even outside the princely houses. "Oriental" became synonomous with "Turkish", and the use of oriental carpets began to spread. They became common even in bourgeois homes.

Turkish carpets retained their enormous popularity for many decades. Only in the latter 19th century, after special historical exhibitions of Persian carpets had been held, were they reassessed: the Turkish carpets stood no comparison with the magnificent pieces of Persian origin loaned by castles and palaces.

The turning point

The general public had had no idea that craft products of such exquisite beauty could be created by human hands. People had been unaware of their existence. During periods of peace and relative well-being in Europe, the merchant houses and carpet-dealers were now overwhelmed with inquiries about carpets. People wanted to buy Persian carpets, and they were willing to pay high prices. Buyers were dispatched to Persia with orders to find and acquire the best carpets they could obtain in the bazaars. Caravan after caravan arrived from Tabriz, where the carpets were collected together, at Constantinople, to be shipped westwards.

In the early stages, the expertise available was minimal. Apart from the pioneers, a few historians of art, only a tiny group of carpet-dealers had much idea about carpets, and this more by way of practical experience than actual knowledge. Suddenly, however, increasing numbers of historians and even more amateurs began to study carpets. "Collecting carpets" became a popular hobby, and a very expensive one. But then the Prophet himself had remarked that only those who could afford it should make the pilgrimage to Mecca.

Those who devoted themselves to this hobby were not disappointed. If they kept their eyes open as well as their wallets, they could get a great deal more for their money than just the carpet. On the space of a few square yards, they could experience into the bargain countless centuries of Eastern poetry, mystery and beauty. Their knowledge increased at a surprising rate, and many amateur collectors contributed by their experience and interpretations to the progress of research.

Before long, the waves of this interest reached the coasts of America, and soon many wealthy collectors on the grand scale had joined the game. Followed by a carpet-minded general public. The demand grew to a level at which it could not be met by the carpets to be found in the bazaars.

To eke out the natural supply, and above all to meet the demand for certain popular sizes — delivery period 3-8 years! — a number of western firms decided to set up workshops in the various districts, each of which would manufacture its own traditional type of carpet. These workshops were furnished with hand-spun yarn, dyed in the same way and with the same vegetable substances as had been used for centuries. Beautiful old carpets lent their patterns for the new, and every detail of manufacture was carefully supervised by reliable inspectors. The new carpets differed from the originals only in their measurements. The Persians themselves preferred long carpets, for their long rooms, the length being about twice the breadth, for example 13ft × 6ft 6in, 16ft 6in × 7ft 6in etc. The measurements now most frequent in the trade, 9ft 9in × 6ft 6in, 13ft × 9ft 9 in etc., are custom measurements. The smaller carpets, on the other hand, retained their original size.

Production, which according to vague estimates amounted to some 10 percent of the country's total carpet exports, continued on a regular basis, and was interrupted only by the two world wars.

Demand, price increases, industrialization

The great upswing in the history of Persian carpets came after World War II. Everywhere, the standard of living gradually rose and people of taste were making greater demands than the factory-manufactured carpets could meet. Neither the natural supply, nor the already forced production of the workshops, could keep pace with the steadily rising demand. The only solution seemed to be to cut the manufacturing time for each carpet by a few months or weeks. As a result, increasing numbers of the cheaper commercial or standard quality were woven, and increasingly few finer carpets. The shortage of the latter soon made itself felt, particularly once the oil sheiks had begun to appear as large-scale buyers on the Persian market. They now consume the best-quality carpets by the square mile, to adorn their own palaces and those of their hundreds of sons.

The supply from millions of private homes — previously the most important source of carpets — began seriously to fail some twenty years after World War II, and what is now left is very much the bottom of the barrel. Many Persians have themselves become collectors, and can be separated from their treasures only by the direst poverty. They realize now how carelessly they have been wasting their carpets all these years, and know the time has passed when showpiece carpets could still be manufactured. The proverb that time in the Orient is not counted in money has long been out of date.

The cost of living is rocketing even in Iran, the present name for Persia. Anyone visiting the country at intervals of a few years notices on each occasion a sharp rise in prices. Soon, it will no longer pay to weave carpets for the low wages paid by the workshops, or for what can be obtained in the bazaars. By way of comparison, it can be mentioned that if Persian workers enjoyed the same wages and benefits as their European and American colleagues, every carpet would cost some 10 to 15 times its present price.

The industrialization of Iran has gathered enormous speed since the mid 50s, and rapid progress is being made. Industry offers a better income than work at the loom, and it can employ many more. The result, it is to be feared, will be the same as everywhere else: a flight to the towns, to the centers of industry. The breaking up of the big estates drew many families from the looms out into their own fields, and the reorganization of education is also eliminating the cheapest — and best! — labor force, namely the hundreds and thousands of school-age children. In the absence of teachers, students are being sent out to teach in the villages instead of doing their National Service.

The future is not difficult to foresee. In the majority of countries, Persian carpets attract high duties and taxes. If we deduct the markup of the middlemen, transport costs, insurance, washing, repairs and other overheads of the dealers, very little is left over to compensate for the many years' or months' work claimed by the weaving.

The Persians, who are not used to rapid change, believe it will be possible to continue exporting carpets for perhaps another ten years, with a margin of a further seven years for nomad carpets. Western experts familiar with both buying and selling take a more pessimistic view. All in all, the latter are probably right. The Persian carpet will again become the privilege of an exclusive few, who can afford to pay its extremely high price. As soon as Iran, instead of exporting its raw materials and importing back finished products, begins to exploit its own natural resources and process them in its own industries, the story of Persian carpet-weaving will be practically over. Possibly, this may take longer than expected.

In many villages all carpet-weaving has already stopped, the population have obtained work in the factories. The 1962 earthquake wiped out 150 villages in the great carpet-making district around Hamadan. Villages where carpets were woven from sunrise to sunset in every house completely vanished. The bell, we fear, will soon finally have tolled for the most legendary of all craft products.

What Sort of Carpet Should I Choose?

Before going to buy a carpet, you should ask the following questions:
1. How big should it be?
2. In what *milieu* is it to be placed: living-room, dining-room, bed-room etc.?
3. What colors are the furniture and curtains in the relevant room?
4. What price am I prepared to pay cash, and what maximum debt am I prepared to incur if credit terms are arranged?

1 The maximum size of a carpet is determined mainly by the space available. However, you must allow a margin of 6−10 in in both directions. You must also be prepared to compromise, as one seldom finds the right colors, the right pattern, the right price *and* the right size. No standard measurements, exact to the last inch exist in the case of Persian carpets.

The majority of carpets sold in the trade are of medium size — c. 6ft 9in × 4ft — since these are easy to place, and not over expensive. Large carpets admittedly give a greater overall impression, but they demand space and are naturally considerably more expensive. On the other hand, no fears need be entertained as regards the handling of large carpets. There is no longer any need to call in outside help for cleaning: regular vacuuming will keep carpets perfectly clean. The beating of carpets is an antiquated procedure, and should be avoided since it can cause serious damage to them.

The sizes generally occurring are as follows:

Miniature carpets	c.	2 ft 9 in × 2 ft	in Persian	:	Poshti
Baby	"	" 4 ft × 2 ft 8 in	" "	:	Zarcharak
Small	"	" 5 ft × 3 ft 3 in	" "	:	Zaronim
Canapé	"	" 6 ft 6 in × 3 ft 3 in	" "	:	Tachtekabi
Medium	"	" 6 ft 9 in × 4 ft	" "	:	Dozar
Suite	"	" 7 ft 3 in × 5 ft	" "	:	Sezar
Large	"	" 9 ft 9 in × 6 ft 6 in and upwards	" "	:	Ghali
Extra large	"	" 21 ft 4 in × 14 ft 9 in and upwards	" "	:	Ghali bozorg
Gallery/runner	"	" 13 ft × 3 ft	" "	:	Kenare
Exotic	"	" 16 ft 6 in × 6 ft	" "	:	Kellegi

Many other measurements exist, including 6 × 6 ft, 8 ft 6 in × 6 ft etc., but have no special name.

The Persian "zar" is really a measure of length, corresponding to about 3ft 5in. In the context of carpets, however, it is accepted as a unit of surface measure, a "square zar". Dozar means two zar. A dozar carpet is thus about 24 sq ft, but in fact it is always slightly larger. Sezar means three zar. A carpet of this size is thus about 36 sq ft. "Zarcharak" and "zaronim" designate sizes of about 11 and 16 sq ft, while "tachtekabi" means sleeping-mat size. "Poshti" comes from "posht", which is Persian for back. Hard cushion to support the back are sewn from these small carpets. If then, as happens, you see a carpet advertised as, say, a "Dozar", it is a measurement designation, not a designation of origin.

Miniature and small carpets can be attractive in front of small pieces of funiture, or over a bald patch in the room, but to cover a large floor surface only with small "tiles", however picturesque it may sound, will never give an elegant effect. Excessively large carpets are impractical; it's a bad thing to put, say, one leg of a cupboard on the corner of the carpet. An excessively small dining-room carpet is equally impractical. Every time you sit down to table, the carpet rolls under the back legs of your chair.

Tell the salesman what room the carpet is to furnish. Mention whether it is to lie free, or under a piece of furniture. **2**

A carpet with a "mirror-frame" medallion on a coloured background loses in aesthetic effect if the medallion is partly covered by an arm-chair or other furniture. On the other hand, carpets with an all-over design function equally well under furniture as lying free.

These are no dogmas. The hundreds and thousands of different patterns in existence and the many different approaches to furnishing make it impossible to give definite rules. Nor are such rules desirable.

Understandably enough, you will want to achieve a harmony between the textiles in your home. Although the basic color or "ground" of almost 98 percent of all Persian carpets, is red, blue or beige, there are so many other shades inwoven in each carpet that some of them will surely match or offset your curtains and furniture fabric. **3**

Textiles in single colors will go with practically any carpet. With striking, flowered fabrics choose sober carpets with calm surfaces, either with an all-over design or small medallions on a plain background. If you have any sample pieces of fabrics used in the room, take them along. If you are still doubtful, ask to have the carpet sent home on approval so that you can judge it in the right *milieu*.

The majority of interior decorators choose the carpet first and then the textiles. They, like the orientals, see carpets as the very basis of a home.

No commentary should really be necessary, since one must assume that the buyer himself knows best how far he or she can go. However, the temptation of seeing the piles of carpets that some shops have to offer can be too much. Ask to start the demonstration from the lowest price ranges upwards. When you have reached the price you have in mind, don't be embarrassed to say that that's the limit. Carpets are heavy things to handle, and the salesman will be only too grateful not to have to demonstrate a whole lot unnecessarily.

On Buying a Carpet

A carpet should never be bought on impulse.

You will start, perhaps, by studying the advertisements of different firms to obtain advance information, comparing types, sizes and prices, and often ending up fairly disorientated. Partly because the prices vary so amazingly for carpets of roughly the same size, partly because the names are so confusing that you are not certain whether they are the same types of carpet or not. You will soon realize that carpets, with a few exceptions, are named after the town from which they come, or the tribe that has made them. The firms, however, spell these names entirely differently, depending which form and orthography they use of those current: the English, the German etc. They may reproduce the wrongly spelled version of the Persian supplier, who is not used to writing Latin letters and perhaps has hardly any command of the foreign language. The result is that the same carpet can be called Jowzan, Dschoschan, Djosan — or something completely different.

You will also discover fairly soon that the carpets described so attractively in the advertisements by no means come up to expectation. The salesman who notices a customer's disappointment will cheerfully demonstrate a better carpet — which will naturally be more expensive. And another and another. The same scene is repeated in other shops. Everywhere, you write up the name, number, measurement and price of the carpets — and when you get home, you have no idea which or them was which.

It *is* difficult for a layman to judge the relative merits of the carpets he sees in different shops. The "facts" given can vary unbelievably, according to the salesman's expertise or imagination. A wealth of unfamiliar names and data tell you nothing. The confused customer begins to realize that in the absence of even an elementary knowledge of oriental carpets, he is in a helplessly exposed position on the market.

What advice can I give you? Read the professional literature, and go and look in shop windows! Learn as much as you can about carpets! If you know carpets, you can buy any carpet. If you are unsure of yourself, turn to a solid reliable firm, in which you have confidence. You won't get the carpet free, but you can at least be sure of getting value from money, not just a worthless guarantee that the carpet comes from this and that place — which is by no means always certain.

Acquire a knowledge of carpets!

Reliability has nothing to do with the size of a firm. It will be reflected rather in their sober advertisements, in their window display, in the boldness of their price tags, and above all in the correct behavior and expert knowledge of their salesmen. In your noticing they want to help you, and are not simply concerned to persuade you to buy the first carpet you happen to point to.

Above all, watch out for firms promising discounts of up to 50 percent. There is every reason to suspect a firm that can cut its prices by this amount. One is bound to ask what mark-up they had been reckoning with, if they *really can* make discounts of this kind. *Buying a carpet cheaply is not the same thing as buying a cheap carpet!*

You can also ignore such advertising boasts as "Own direct import" or "Recently returned from a purchasing tour of Persia" etc. This is no guarantee of a favorable deal. Numerous buyers have made fatal purchases in the Orient. The bazaar has its own moral code, its own unwritten laws that you have to know. You must never be in a hurry, bargaining is a ritual that takes its time. Credit and fixed prices are non-existent. To pay the price demanded without haggling would be "unfair". To haggle too little makes the seller suspicious. Perhaps he undervalued the carpet. Best not to sell . . . If you haggle too much, you will be ranted at, and pierced through and through by the darkest of glances. The carpet-sellers of the bazaar know all the tricks, and the buyer from a far-off country has to be a very good hand at the game to provide worthy opposition to these native champions. — Also, if the expensive journey to the Orient is to pay off, you have to have a great deal of both cash and time at your disposal.

There is little chance of making a find in the dinky, junk-shop type places in Western countries. These usually stick to simpler carpets, among which it is rare indeed to see a quality product.

The large, respectable auction companies of international repute try to maintain a certain standard when they accept carpets for sale, but they do not always have the experts available carefully to investigate all that comes their way. This is something you must do yourself when they are on display. As a rule, the auctioneers will not be held responsible for any shortcomings.

The carpet auctions that are regularly held are really only another way of selling carpets. If the pre-set price is not reached, the carpet is bought back by one of the firm's own representatives and put up at the next auction. The competitive spirit — a spirit often bordering on hysteria — can push prices at an auction up, so that a carpet will cost far more than it would in a shop.

Inspect the carpet carefully!

Investigate: 1. If the carpet is worn. 2. If it is moth-eaten. 3. If it is brittle. Easiest to discover is the wear: the pile will be gone, and the warp threads visible in places. However, the white warp threads may have been painted over as camouflage.

To locate all the moth-eaten patches that may exist, it is necessary to investigate the carpet carefully, inch by inch. If the moths have been content to attack a few small places on the front of the carpet, there is no imminent danger. There is, on the other hand, if they have banqueted on the reverse side! If the loops of the knots on the back of the carpet are eaten, the pile on the front can be picked off more easily than plucking a chicken. So study the back of the carpet! Any bald, moth-eaten patches may have been painted over, and be difficult to discover. The back of a carpet will also betray any repairs, both large and small, particularly if they are makeshifts.

Your most careful investigation, however, should be for brittleness. If a carpet has been damaged by water, perhaps by sea-water during transport, it is practically worthless. It will quickly fall to pieces at the brittle places as soon as you use it. This is how to check for brittleness. Fold the carpet lengthwise, with the pile inwards. Hold it between two fingers of each hand, and carefully try to fold it again. If it "crackles", the warp and weft threads are brittle and will break even from this slight bending. Repeat the procedure at several places. Be careful to fold the carpet gently and cautiously! If you use your full strength, even the strongest carpet can break.

At estate auctions, anything can happen. If you have no knowledge of carpets, it would be ridiculous to bid more than what a machine-made carpet is worth — this may be just what it is.

If you have difficulty in deciding on *one* of several carpets you like, use a process of elimination.

Place the carpets beside each other on the floor. Take away the one you like least, turn away for a moment so that you will get a fresh impression of those remaining. Eliminate the one you like least! And so on, until only one — the right one — remains.

Should you change your mind, it is an advantage to have bought your carpet from a respectable firm. There, you can always arrange to exchange your carpet for another. In many cases, it is perfectly possible to find another carpet in the same price range as the first; experience, however, shows that people usually exchange *upwards,* paying a bit more money.

See that the invoice includes a clause "Free right of exchange within 30 days"! Obviously, when the carpet is returned it must be in the same condition as when supplied by the firm.

Prices

You are standing before two Persian carpets, equally large and of the same type; even the pattern is fairly similar. One of them, however, costs five times as much as the other. Why?

The price is determined by four factors:

1. The beauty of the carpet: its artistic combination of pattern and colors.
2. Its quality: how closely woven it is, the nature of the wool and dyes used.
3. Its age: is it recently manufactured, some years old, or really old, with the patina of age?
4. Its condition: what state is it in, how well preserved is it?

The most important price-determining factor is the beauty of a carpet, its visual effect. **1**

Quality comes in second place, although it helps to make a carpet attractive. Higher qualities permit more delicate patterns than coarser qualities. **2**

By quality we mean the closeness of the weave, the number of knots per square inch. The back of a carpet is a sort of work-sheet: it tells us how many months or years its manufacture took, and whether the loom was worked by a master or a novice. The number of knots varies enormously between different types and qualities, from about 40 up to 500 or even more per square inch. We must emphasize at this point that *it is impossible to compare the quality of two different types of carpet on the basis of the number of knots*. Certain types of carpet will be classified as outstanding if they have some 50 knots per sq in, while others are only mediocre although they have 150 knots per sq in.

The quality of the wool is of great importance. Better quality wool gives a more attractive appearance. There are several sorts of wool in Persia, with different properties according to the breed of sheep, the shifting climate, height above sea level and the nutritional value of the pasture. Wool from Kurdistan is tough and lustreless. Shiraz wool is soft, as is that of Kirman and Meshed, with plenty of animal fat in the fibres to give a high gloss. Tabriz carpets feel rougher when you stroke them with your palm, because the Azerbaijan area has quite another type of wool. The softest wool of all is called "kork" and it is also the most expensive. It comes from Merino sheep, and is imported from Australia or New Zealand, mainly for the very finest Kashan carpets.

Do not confuse the lustre of a carpet with its quality! Nain and Isfahan carpets, for instance, which are recognized to have the tightest weave of all, have but little lustre. On carpets from other districts, the long woollen fibres of the pile are worn down until they are of equal length, and lie tightly packed against each other to reflect the light. Since each district has used, over the centuries, the yarn spun from its own wool, the character of the carpets has developed according to the properties of the wool, which have demanded different techniques of dying and knotting.

The color composition is influenced by the local plants, from which the dyes are made. Since the color of the newly dyed yarn is fairly garish, the great importance of the carpet's quality appears only after some years of use. With time, the colors change, becoming milder and more subtle. In this way, the carpets acquire their inimitable tone.

3   As a rule, older carpets are more valuable than new. They are rarer, their patterns deviate more often from those seen on more recent products, and they have had time to acquire a certain patina. The difference between an old carpet and a new is much the same as that between an 18th century chest-of-drawers, and one on which the varnish is just dry.

Such concepts as "old", "semi-antique" and "antique" are extremely vague. In ten carpet shops, you will get ten different answers. The historian of art will consider as antique only carpets manufactured in the 18th century or earlier. The trade, and Customs officials, set the limit rather later. They classify all carpets over a century old as antique, and thus exempt from duty. If we accept this argument, we can set up the following model:

Antique carpets	over	100 yrs old
Semi-antique carpets	over	60 yrs old
Old carpets	between 25 —	60 yrs old

"Semi-old" means simply a *used* carpet up to about 25 years old, without any noticeable patina.

People assume that the carpets sold in shops are faultless. As a rule, **4** they are. But exceptions can occur. Sometimes, a carpet can have acquired a small nick during transport, for instance from a hook, or being too tightly folded so that the weft treads have broken. These are minor injuries that can be repaired without difficulty, and not even the repairer will afterwards be able to find the fault. Nor does it matter if the carpet has a small hole, or is slightly damaged by moth. New knots in place of those missing are sewn of carefully selected yarn, dyed to exactly the right shade. *A properly repaired carpet will have recovered its full value.*

If a carpet has been repaired in *several* places its value *decreases* accordingly, even if the repairs are visible only on the back.

In the case of antique and semi-antique carpets, one can assume that they will have been repaired over the years — these repairs being but the scars on the toreador's body. If these mends have been skilfully performed, and have aged for some years with the carpet itself, the decline in value will be minimal. If they are clumsily executed, too recent, or too obvious, the value of the carpet will fall accordingly.

It is also obvious that a carpet of medium quality will be worn to some extent after 50 years of normal use. If it is *evenly worn over the entire surface,* it is still perfect. A carpet, on the other hand, that is worn in patches has lost *much of its value.* Such carpets are extremely difficult to repair satisfactorily.

An antique or semi-antique carpet whose pattern is still clearly visible, although the pile is almost completely gone, can still have its value for the collector, or the historian of art. Fifty- or sixty-year-old carpets that are greatly worn have neither an historical or practical value. When the warp begins to wear, large holes can occur as soon as they are used again. Hung on a wall, however, they can be extremely decorative.

Aniline, dyes, ink or other spots on a carpet *reduce* its value.

It is not as easy to remove spots from an oriental carpet as it is to remove coffee stains from a table-cloth. Usually, you don't even know what sort of stain it is, or whether it has been fixated by some previous attempt to remove it. So never believe assurances, perhaps made in all good faith, that "it'll easily go away". Ask the salesman to arrange that particular detail himself *before* you decide to buy. To be on the safe side, it is always wise to follow this piece of oriental advice: "Before leaving your camel to the protection of Allah, bind it firmly to the fence."

The Symbols

Don't buy a story! Don't waste a lot of money simply because a smart salesman has tried to make a carpet more desirable with an apocryphal story. "Stolen from a mosque", "The Shah gave it to last ambassador", "It's from the Aga Khan's collection", "It comes from a harem" and similar stories are as ancient as they are untruthful. Let the carpets tell their own story!

Magic and superstition are deeply entrenched in Asia, and the belief in the One God has failed to uproot them. The dethroned household gods have been replaced by amulets and symbols designed to bring good fortune, or avert bad. This tradition has transplanted itself vigorously from generation to generation, over thousands of years. Below are some of the most common symbols to be found on carpets.

The *fish* is a symbol of family happiness. Large numbers of children meant more available labor, greater wealth, status for the tribe. In the case of the best-known version, the "Herati" pattern, it is questionable whether the fish is not in fact an *acanthus leaf*. The pattern was called after the city of Herat in Afghanistan, the 13th century stronghold of Islam. It consists of a rhomb flanked by four fishes. It is also known as the "Feraghan" pattern, after the Persian city which specialized in this motif.

Another symbol of family happiness is the *duck*.

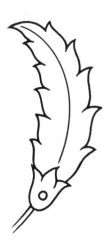

Left: Fish or acanthus leaf
Right: Herati or Feraghan pattern

The Tree of Life. In the Orient, where water is in short supply, a tree in bloom was the symbol of vital force. The father of the family identified himself with the trunk of the tree, his progeny with the branches. European Crusaders adopted this image, which has persisted in the West to our own days in the form of the "family tree".

The Tree of Life is to found in countless variations, from gorgeous trees of paradise from the royal workshops to naivist designs from the nomad camps.

The *tortoise* symbolizes — and is intended to further — a long life. The cemeteries of the Orient contain far more children than adults. Those who reach an advanced age are considered to be Allah's favorites. Hence some of the respect accorded to age.

The very primitively drawn *falcon* that you often see on carpets from the Hamadan district is a fertility symbol of Mesopotamian origin, dating back many thousands of years. According to legend, the falcon flew into a great tree, whose seed fell down to fertilize the world.

The *hour-glass* has retained its importance in Asia. A reminder that no one can escape. This theme is found almost exclusively on carpets from the Caucasian and Turkish frontier areas.

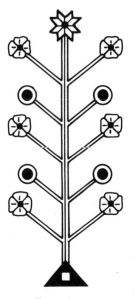

Tree of Life

Falcon

Hour glass

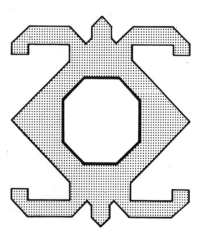

Versions of the tortoise

26

The *cloud ribbon* is perhaps the most graceful of all the ornaments which adorn a carpet. Known in China as "tchi" it is a symbol of good fortune. The original tchi, however, resembles more a mother-of-pearl shell or cirrus cloud. It is possible that the *Persian* cloud ribbon was modelled on *Omega,* the most beautiful letter in the Greek alphabet.

The *Running Dog* is the amusing name given to a softer version of the meander which decorated the chitons or tunics of Greek soldiers. The heavy, rectilinear meander is extremely rare. It never really fitted in with the graceful flora of Persian patterns.

The *recumbent S* with a dividing line in the middle has long defied all attempts at interpretation. In actual fact, it is a question of the letter D in the Armenian alphabet. D stands for Dios, or God. Many Christian Armenians were forcibly transported some centuries ago from their own country to Persia, where they have since comprised small ethnic and religious islands in the great sea of Islam. The Armenians were outstanding carpet-weavers, and continued their activities in their new home. Their carpets were bought mainly by Moslems, who used them as prayer carpets. The Armenians therefore knotted in the first letter of God's name, and decorated their carpets also with the Cross. The Moslem carpet-weavers, who were often ignorant even of the Arabic letters, took over these S's as ornaments, using them in borders as a chain, or scattered assymmetrically over the central field. Today, the meaning of this ornamentation has been forgotten even by the Armenians.

Running dog

Recumbent S, two versions

Crenellated design

The *palmette* is one of the classical decorative designs. The leaves are arranged in the shape of a fan around a solid nucleus, and curved at the top. Since the Ionic and Corinthian columns were adorned with a similar ornament — the anthemion — it has been assumed that the palmette is also of Greek origin. More likely is that it was modeled on the cut fruit-vessel of the opium poppy! The poppy stems from Persia, and it was known, cultivated, used and abused even in early times. It is easy to imagine that it once had a magical or religious import. The leaves may have been added purely for decoration.

The *weeping willow* and the *cypress* are the symbols of grief and death. The eternally green cypress is also a reminder of the life after death.

The *Star of Solomon* actually has nothing to do with the wise king. When the Hittite ruins at Ortaköy near Constantinople were excavated in the 20's, an imperial sign was found suspended over each royal name, the Star of Solomon, with two eagle's wings. This star is extremely common on certain Anatolian and Caucasian carpets. It was introduced to Persia by the Kurds, although it reached only to Hamadan.

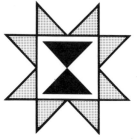

The Star of Solomon

The interesting thing is that the royal emblem of a people who vanished from the arena of world history some 3,000 years ago was never forgotten. It bears the name it does because King Solomon is held in high esteem by the Mohammedans, and because the emblem resembles the Star of David. It thus seemed natural to name it after King David's son and successor.

Cypress

Weeping willows

28

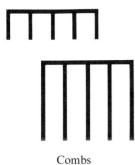

Combs

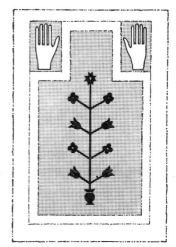 *(water-jug image)*

Water-jug

The *hand with fingers extended* is to be seen in the upper corners of certain prayer carpets of the Belouch tribe. The five fingers symbolize the holy pentad of the Shiite sect: Mohammed, his daughter Fatima, his grandson the Iman Ali, and his two martyred nephews Hussein and Hassan.

The *comb* is not in reality a comb at all, but symbolises the "pillars of the Faith", the five pillars on which Islam rests.

The *water-jug* is a religious attribute, since washing of the fingertips is part of the Mohammedan ritual. It is thus an image of purity. Also, its slim shape and narrow pipe prevent wastage of the water.

Mir or Mir i botah, which means "princely flower", is the most familiar of all designs. No other design has been interpreted in so many different ways. Here are some of the interpretations:

It portrays a flame. Fire signified purification in Zoroastrian Persia, where self-priming natural gas constantly flared up from the barren earth. Finding no explanation for the phenomenon, the Persians ascribed great mystical properties to the flames.

It is a seal, the impression of a hand. Princes were accustomed to impress the edge of the closed fist, dipped in blood, on documents to seal an agreement. The resulting mark resembled the "Mir".

The pattern of the Crown Jewels. The old crown of the Shah had a Mir arrangement at the front, richly adorned with jewels.

It is a winding of the Indus.

It has been suggested that "Mir" may be an abbreviation of Kashmir. Kashmir shawls bearing only the mir pattern were extremely popular in Europe before and after the turn of the century.

Cypress in the storm, the pear, the womb, the fir-cone, the leaf, these are some of the alternative names arrived at by subjective association.

Another possibility is that the design stems from China, and that

Two versions of the Mir or Mir i botah

Hands and Tree of Life

it had, in its original form, great significance. The Yin-Yang cycle symbolizes male and female propagation. The Persians of olden days were well aware of its meaning. Among good Moslems, men and women never sat together. They separated the Yin-Yang cycle, the two halves of which suddenly became two "Mir"! The profaned symbol no longer tempted the faithful to unworthy thoughts. To render these carpets still more acceptable in the mosques, the Mir was so applied that one row slopes to the left and another to the right. So far as is known, they were always arranged in this manner on the older carpets.

The Yin-Yang cycle

It is easy to understand how flowers and plants can become the symbols for magical concepts, since natural peoples have always used plants in preparing their medicines, poisons, love potions, drugs etc. While the "flower language" of the West is very simple, that of the East is shrouded in mystery.

The *Assyrian rose* expresses not only unsatisfied longing, but also the magic number 7 since it flowers for seven years.

Jasmin is the flower of expectation; the loins of the houris in Paradise have the fragrance of jasmin.

The *tulip* symbolizes hypocrisy; straight and attractively noble when closed, but with a black heart . . .

The *almond blossom* is the flower of youth. The flower of love and longing. Two almond kernels in one shell are associated with two young heads on the same pillow.

The *evil eye* and its magic power are very much a reality to Easterners, who are terrified of jealous, malicious looks, convinced that they can cause misfortunes. Turquoise beads are a good protection for both livestock and humans . . . Small multi-colored tassels embroidered along the short side of a carpet are also effective, as are small secret, extremely private signs or figures woven into the centre field.

Seemingly unwarranted deviations in the pattern of old, high-quality carpets can also mean that the pious and humble weaver was concerned to avoid encroaching upon Allah's privilege of creating something perfect. Probably the warp threads are also odd in number, since Allah is one. Safest, of course, would be to weave in the name of the Imam Ali, or the martyr Hussein — provided you can write . . . A rare carpet of this kind is to be found from time to time among the early nomad products. On the other hand, the assymmetry of pattern to be found in nomad carpets — with ornamental designs or figures that have been started, but not finished — was not the result of superstition. This charming irregularity was caused by moving camp.

The *arabesque,* an elegantly curved, plant-like flourish, is the Arabian contribution to Persian decorative art. It was probably modelled on the acanthus leaf so frequently used for decorative purposes by Byzantine artists.

Arabesques

The Arabs developed decorative art into a superbly varied surface ornamentation, an ingenious play of lines in which the pattern was continually repeated by the rythmic interweaving of contours in each other. They also carried the art of calligraphy to near perfection, and Arabic characters could be incorporated in the coiling lines without disrupting either the basic pattern or the harmony of the lines. Arabic ornamentation never represents any images beyond the actual characters, which always have a meaning.

The *anchor medallion* is to be found only in Persian Kurdistan. We do not know if it has any special meaning, but it makes it much easier to identify the provenance of a carpet.

The more common *bar medallion,* mainly from the Hamadan district, ends in two arrowheads. The arrowhead is the symbol of a readiness to fight, a declaration of strength, and was also a means of furthering good luck in the hunt.

Persian carpets are pregnant with symbols. If, at the time of buying, you learn very little of the cultural and historical content that is undoubtedly present in your carpet, then study for yourself the religious concepts, ornamentation and symbolism of these ancient cultures. To discover for yourself the "messages" communicated by your carpet will give you enormous pleasure.

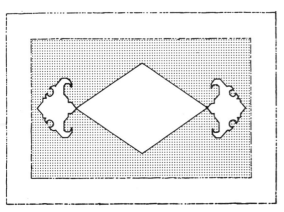

Anchor medallion

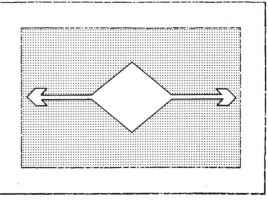

Bar medallion

The Dyes

From time immemorial, people have used plants and other organic substances to color their yarns and fabrics. In Persia, the experience of countless generations has been stewarded by a guild which carried the art of dyeing to a perfection encountered nowhere else in the world.

Dyeing the yarn involves far more than dipping it in a color solution. It has to be washed, and the wool fibers may have to be freed from excess animal fat so that the dye will penetrate. Mixing the right shade, boiling the yarn for a specific time, balancing the necessary salt and acid additives and rinsing — rinsing in a tub is very different from rinsing in running water! All this involves a very careful procedure.

We often speak of "natural" and "artificial" dyes.

By *natural* dyes we mean the *organic* dyes extracted from indigo, saffron, madder root, henna, bark, fruit peel, different plant leaves etc. Dyes are also obtained from several animal substances, including cochineal, the attractive red color produced from the dried and pounded females of the cochineal-insect, and purple, which is secreted by the gland of mollusks of the genus Purpura. Purple was famous even in ancient times.

By *artificial* dyes we mean *synthetic* dyes. The first synthetic dyes, evolved in the mid 19th century, were produced from a waste product of coal tar. Subsequent development was rapid, since the synthetic dyes made the Western countries independent of expensive tropical plants.

It was soon the turn of the European manufacturers to sell dyes to the Orient, thus reversing a traffic that had lasted for many centuries. The Persians, too, were impressed by the new dyes, but they could not use them properly. Although the procedure to be used with synthetic dyes was much simpler, the yarn was still treated as it always had been. The result was devastating. The carpets looked awful, and exports fell catastrophically — as did the reputation of Persian carpets. The government took drastic action, and confiscated the carpets in which new dyes had been used.

The dye masters soon came to their senses. The merchants in the bazaars refused to pay even half what they had paid for the old carpets. Also, they had the majority of dyes available free in their own back yard. It was a simple matter of going out into the country and picking them. Indigo, on the other hand, was imported from India and it was expensive. Madder could also be expensive when there was a drought, and the root was not filled with the usual fine red substance. These were the only two colors it was worth replacing, with synthetic indigo and alizarin, which is a synthesis of madder.

On colors that "last"

The adjectives "natural" and "artificial" can be misleading. It has been widely believed that natural dyes *last*, while artificial dyes *lose their color*. The truth is that today's synthetic dyes are light-resistent and washable, they faithfully retain their original shade of color indefinitely. This is just what is wrong with them! If a carpet manufactured of synthetically dyed yarn is cleaned after many years of use, it will look like new. Vegetable dyes, on the other hand, *change* their original shades with the effects of light and age. The colors lose their sharpness, and are toned down to inimitably attractive shades. In this property lies the whole secret and magic of vegetable dyes. This is what gives carpets with age the same patina as old silver or furniture. If you look between the pile of an old carpet, you can clearly see how much harder the colors are at the bottom, where the light has not penetrated.

Naturally, carpets are still made exclusively of yarn treated with vegetable dyes. This applies particularly to the higher qualities, where the saving made by using cheaper yarn would be negligible in relation to the carpet's price. Countless proud carpet-weavers mix their own dyes. This procedure, like the pattern, has been handed down in the family. The same is true of certain nomad tribes, who are self-supporting as regards materials. They shear their own sheep, spin the wool, and dye the yarn with plants from around the camp. Since the vegetation varies from one part to another, different scales of color were developed by each tribe, giving their carpets an individual character.

We can assume that the yarn used in the very cheapest carpets is treated exclusively with synthetic dyes. The better carpets will have one or two colors not from an organic substance. The dye masters, however, seldom use the standard dyes without giving them a personal touch, adding vegetable dyes that will give life to the carpet.

The symbolism of colors. Abrash carpets

The colors, too, have their symbolism. The color of grief varies from black in England, via red in the Vatican and mauve in Armenia to white in China. In the world of Islam, green is a greatly revered color since Mohammed's banner was green. The Hadjis, those who have made the pilgrimage to Mecca, and the Saids, the descendants of the Prophet, wear a green turban and green girdle. Previously, it would have been unthinkable to weave a green carpet, and it is rare to find any shades of green in old carpets. This taboo is no longer respected. Otherwise, the favorite colors of the Oriental are orange, the color of religious submission, and turquoise. If a carpet has a belt of another shade, this has nothing to do with superstition. The yarn came to an end while work was in progress, and new skeins had to be dyed. There was no clock available, and the sun perhaps went behind a cloud — the yarn has been boiled for a slightly longer or shorter time, and become somewhat darker or lighter. These "abrash" carpets are in great demand among collectors. They can be extremely attractive and spontaneous. And you can be sure that they were manufactured for own use, not for export.

Reliable experts have estimated the synthetic dyes used in Persia at only 10 percent of the total dye consumed. This, quantitatively, is not much — but it is still too much. No chemist can produce such attractive colors as the Almighty Himself.

Illustrative Carpets

The Koran contains no prohibition against depicting living creatures. Among the traditionally-minded Sunnites, however, the art of pictorial representation is taboo, since it might tempt people to worship images. Thus we find no pictures on Turkish or Arabian carpets. The Persian are Shiites, their artists have not been hampered by bigotry. Throughout the ages, they have created fabulous carpets, miniature paintings, book illustrations, ceramics and silverware, in which the representation of people and animals is an essential decorative element.

Hunting carpets are miniature paintings projected on a surface of several square yards. The horsemen with their curved sabres or drawn bows, the flying manes of the Mongolian horses, the movements of the fleeing deer, all these are caught in the hundredth of a second in which their perfect beauty and dynamic movement best come to expression. The same applies to the classical animal carpets in which wild beasts engage in mortal combat, cruel yet fascinating in their remorselessly primitive state.

The ruins of Persepolis are a never-failing source of inspiration. The columns and the reliefs on the ruined walls, which neither Alexander's fist nor the tooth of time have been able to expunge, are frequent motifs. Above all, the king's battle with the winged, eagle-clawed lion.

The worship of kings and heroes has always been close to the oriental heart. The legendary King Djamshid lives on, sitting with dignity on his uncomfortable throne as a servant fans him. Shah Abbas, with his magnificent moustaches, is often depicted, as is his famous creation the Shah Mosque in Isfahan. Or Nadir Shah, sitting on his priceless Peacock Throne, which he brought home from India as a trophy of war.

Many are the dignitaries whose features have been thought worthy of commemoration by devoted carpet-weavers, but there seems no point in recalling further names. The only exception is a fat young lad, Ahmed Shah, who ascended the throne of Persia in the beginning of this century.

The portraits of kings and khans are usually placed in small medallions in the border of a carpet. It is a credit to the Persian sense of proportion that the central field is reserved for one of the country's four most famous authors: Firdausi, Omar al Khayyam, Sadi and Hafiz, to give them in chronological order. Such is the honor paid by a predominantly illiterate people to greatness of the spirit. Have not these authors created works more lasting with their pens, than the kings with their sabres?

Firdausi founded his immortal reputation with a grandiose epic poem on the early Iranian kings. Omar al Khayyam was a brilliant mathematician and astronomer. While devoting his thoughts to the problems of eternity, he urged people, in his poems, to enjoy the present. If we see a picture of a bearded old man attended by a plump brunette with a jug of wine, we can bet ten to one that this is Omar the "tent-maker". Sadi, the aesthete from Shiraz, taught people in his prose and poetry the ethics of justice, love and humility. Many of his stories and anecdotes are still in world circulation today, 700 years after his death. Hafiz was a mystic and master of language, a poet by the grace of Allah who is considered to have written the most beautiful love poems in the world's literature. He, too, is often portrayed in the company of a plump lady, but without a wine jug.

The dervishes are depicted in colorful clothes, a silver axe in their hand and a bejewelled begging-bowl in front of them. But then they are not ordinary beggars, they are spiritual aristocrats. Many of them were extremely wealthy men who voluntarily renounced their riches, mastering themselves and thus the entire world.

The Biblical narratives have provided another source of inspiration. The following Biblical themes are to be found on carpets.

Abraham is ready to sacrifice his son, but is prevented by the angels. The text speaks not of Isaac, but of Ishmael, son of Hagar, whom the Arabs regard as the father of their tribe. The Persians are not Arabs, as they are concerned to emphasize in all possible contexts. But they took over with Islam the legend of the origins of the Prophet's fellow-countrymen.

Another popular theme is that of Joseph and Potiphar's wife.

Joseph is regarded as a sort of Adonis, at the same time the embodiment of piety and righteousness. Djami, Persia's last classic writer, wrote a poetic drama about the couple, entitled Jusuf and Zuleika, the production of which made the character of Joseph still more popular.

King Solomon makes a frequent appearance. Visual motifs are his ingenious decision regarding the true mother of the baby, his encounter with the Queen of Sheba, and his ability to speak the language of animals.

The dramatic story of Samson and Delilah provides food for thought, and inscriptions of the following type can be found: "The man who drinks too much loses not only his hair, but his dignity, his reason, his power and his woman."

The Madonna and Child is a less frequent motif. It occurs, however, as do other themes from the New Testament. They are not taboo. Islam recognizes Christ as *one* of the prophets who preceded Mohammed, but considers that His and all other prophets' missions and importance ended with the appearance of Mohammed as the last prophet and founder of the religion.

One might imagine that the founder of Islam, this sometime camel-driver whose life was so full of dramatic episodes, would be the person most portrayed on carpets. This, however, is not the case. His picture is never seen on a carpet. In later miniatures and book illustrations, he is never portrayed other than with a halo around his turban, and without a face. When Moses descended from Sinai with the tablets, his face was bathed in a supernatural light. He was forced to cover his features, so that the people could raise their eyes towards him. This, probably, gave rise to the view of Moslem artists that it was impossible to portray the face of the Prophet.

In the pastoral themes, all drama is prohibited. Fair summer meadows, browsing sheep, watchful shepherds, long-legged water-fowl, stags, peacocks and a well are conjured forth on these carpets. Or else the central field is a single, impenetrable foliage with small birds hidden among the branches, leaves and flowers. These birds are given camouflaging colors, it can take a long time before you find them all.

Such legendary animals as human-headed serpents, winged lions with the heads of elephants, and dragons, together with water buffalo, elephants, monkeys and other alien fauna testify to an Indian and Chinese influence. These grotesque and mystical animals have practically vanished from more recent Persian carpets.

Mashahir is the name given to a carpet portraying 54 great men of history. The gallery of portraits starts with Adam and continues with, among others, Noah, Abraham, Moses, Alexander the Great, Julius Caesar, Christ and Genghis Khan up to Napoleon and Admiral Nelson. Such a work is more of a curiosity than an attractive oriental carpet.

Example of an illustrative carpet. This is the Mouchtashemi-Kashan, named after Kashan's most famous carpet-weaver. The pictures and text in the surrounding borders tell the story of Jusuf and Zuleika, i.e. Joseph and Potiphar's wife. Jusuf can be seen furthest right, in the uppermost field. Zuleika is sitting furthest down in the middle of the lower field. The ladies are so fired by Jusuf's beauty that some of them are cutting their hands, instead of the fruit. The picture also shows how men and women dine separately, as is still the custom of the East.

Chahar fasl, the four seasons, is one of the most interesting motifs to be composed in the past few centuries. It consists of four pictures, each of them an allegory of the seasons in Azerbaijan. These carpets are manufactured practically only in Tabriz, and are greatly prized. This applies particularly to the thin, early carpets whose borders consist of further allegories, not only ornamentation.

These are only a fraction of the themes and motifs to be found on Persian carpets. Famous mosques, holy tombs, dancing girls, falconing, young noblemen playing polo, attractive jugs and vessels from excavations, and a thousand other objects and illustrations alluding to legends and stories unknown to us, all these appear on carpets.

On the carpets made by nomads, and in nameless small villages, we often see naively drawn camels, rams, ducks, cocks and storks, knotted in here and there with no thought of symmetry. Superstition or playfulness, it makes no difference: such carpets are to be appreciated for their very primitiveness and naive charm.

Regrettably, fine illustrative carpets are becoming increasingly rare, and we must assume that they will soon no longer be made.

Inscriptions

Nothing gives the carpet-lover greater pleasure than to find an inscription or a date, or both, on his carpet. The knotting in of a text was probably practised even in 13th century Herat, although the world's most famous carpet with an inscription and date is the Ardebil carpet from c. 1540 in the Victoria and Albert Museum.

It is an erroneous belief that the inscriptions are verses from the Koran. Carpets with a text from the Koran are extremely rare, and few indeed have crossed the frontiers from the world of Islam. We must comfort ourselves with the hope, if we are lucky, of coming across some of the most exquisite pearls of Persian literature.

To be able to identify all the quotations that have captured the imagination of the carpet-weavers, one would have to be well versed indeed in Persian literature. It is not only the "big four" who are quoted. We can find lines from works by Nizami, Attar, Rumi, Djami and the other classical writers. No other people seem to have accorded such appreciation to the country's great minds as we encounter in Persia. Such quotations are usually framed in attractive cartouches in the main border, the text running around the entire carpet. In rare cases there is an inscription in all three borders, but the carpet is in that case probably of early date and definitely of extremely high quality.

A brief inscription set in stars in all four corners is to be read as "M'borak bad", a form of congratulation and blessing before marriage. These carpets are ordered in advance as wedding presents, and are also called wedding carpets. Early wedding carpets are extremely precious.

The maker's signature is placed as a rule on the upper short side of the carpet, in the middle of the lowermost border. A carpet of this kind has been woven for an exporting workshop. Certain workshops are famous far beyond the frontiers of Persia for their artistic, qualitatively high-standing products. Particularly appreciated are such olden-day masters as Djawan from Tabriz, Arjoman from Kerman, Amoghli from Meshed, Yacoutiel and Mughtashemi from Kashan. Their carpets are nowadays greatly sought after even by the recently awakened Persians. A signature, however, is no guarantee of excellence. Signed carpets of mediocre quality have been appearing in recent years, above all from Tabriz.

The inscription on the *upper* end of an illustrative carpet — in the border or field — is often the name of the person portrayed.

If the writing is on the *lower* end — whether the carpet is illustrative of not — it is probably the name of the customer ordering the carpet.

The lower end is where the carpet was started, its lies *against the pile*.

Kufic is the earliest Arabic form of writing, the rigid lines of which were softened in the 11th century into the present rounder style. It occurs above all in conjunction with pictures of mosques, whose tiled walls are covered with it.

If *cuneic* occurs, it is probably in connection with the reliefs at Behistan, where Darius caused his succession to the throne, and his victories, to be celebrated by rock-carvings. It is thanks to these trilingual inscriptions that cuneic was first interpreted.

Hebraic inscriptions are extremely rare. They consist of such dogmata as: "Hear, O Israel, the Lord our God is One God!". Or the oath of the warriors during the Babylonian captivity: "If I forget Thee, O Jerusalem, let my right hand forget her cunning..." Occasionally, Moses with the tablets or the symbols of the twelve tribes of Israel can be depicted.

The Armenians are excellent carpet-weavers. Although many of them live and work in different districts of Persia, *Armenian* writing is extremely rare on Persian carpets.

Cyrillic and *Latin* inscriptions are to be encountered only on post-war Caucasian and Turkish carpets, respectively. Such carpets lose much of their oriental character, and indeed of their value.

No method of investigation can give as reliable an answer concerning the age of a carpet as an actual date. Strangely enough, dates are more frequent on carpets produced in the small villages and by nomads than on the more cultivated products of the big towns.

Arabic figures offer no difficulties, they take only a few minutes to master. They are, read from left to right:

| 1 | 2 | 3 | 4 | 5 | 6 | 7 | 8 | 9 | 0 |

Dates indicate the year according to the Moslem chronology. This starts from the Hegira, Mohammed's flight from Mecca to Medina in mid July 622. Since the Moslem calendar is based on the 355-day long lunar year, there is a displacement between it and the Gregorian calendar. Dates can easily be converted.

If we take as our example the previously-mentioned Ardebil carpet — dated 946 after the Hegira — then this is how to calculate:

1. The date is divided by 33. The 1/33rd part that distinguishes the solar year from the 11-day shorter lunar year. $946 : 33 = 28.6$.
2. The result is rounded off to the nearest integer, and deducted from the date given on the carpet. $946 - 29 = 917$.
3. Add 622, the year we had reached before the Moslems started counting their year 1. $917 + 622 = 1539$.

The Ardebil carpet was thus completed in 1539 by our chronology.

It can happen that both figures and inscriptions are given in mirror-writing. Such an inscription can easily be read from the back of the carpet.

When buying carpets with inscriptions, ask for the *correct* translation — which is something that should be included in the price! If you already have such a carpet, try to get a faithful translation of the text and find out where it comes from. In this way, you will get a lot more pleasure from your carpet than if you vaguely assume that "it's something from the Koran . . ."

A Mahometan carpet with inscriptions, which reproduce a passage from the Koran. In the corners you find the five holy names of the Mahometans: Mahomet, his daughter Fatima, his son-in-law Ali and their sons Hussein and Hassan. The carpet is on the lower end dated 1322, Mahometan chronology.

The Technique of Weaving Carpets

The manufacture takes place on primitive looms. The type of loom used dates from pre-history, a frame consisting of simple beams around which the warp threads are made tight.

Where the population is settled, the loom is vertical. The weavers sit in front of it, and as work proceeds the seat is raised or the completed part of the carpet rolled up on the lowermost beam. Carpets of any size can be made on these looms. The colored pattern is drawn on a finely chequered paper, each square corresponding to a single knot.

The looms of the nomads are horizontal, and of smaller size. Their mats are thus also smaller, and usually of narrower format. A large loom would be far too inconvenient when moving in the spring and autumn. The weavers sit on their haunches while working, and have no patterns to help them. The nomads have phenomenal memories, they know their own patterns by heart. Their ability to recall is inherited, and further trained by each individual. People who cannot read or write have to be able to remember things. The smallest carpets are the work of *one* person. On the medium and large carpets, two or more weavers work together, predominantly children and women. Each weaver's working field is slightly more than the width of their shoulders, as far as a person can conveniently reach without moving.

If several people are working together on the same carpet, a "teamwork" system is used. No one can glance at the pattern and immediately find the right row, note the right shade of color, and reckon the number of knots. This would be both laborious and confusing. A weaver could easily slip over into his neighbour's working field, and spoil the whole pattern. So a further man is appointed to each loom. This is the Oustad, the Master. It is he who holds the color pattern and keeps work moving smoothly and rapidly. He *sings out* the colors and numbers of knots to the different weavers in different keys. This is how it can sound: "Three red — two beige, one blue — three red — three indigo". None of the four weavers need lift their eyes from their work, they simply follow instructions, taking the right yarn, knotting it, cutting it off. Work proceeds at an unbelievable pace. The singing of the Master lulls the team into a working rythm, which incites at the same time as it sooths. The assuredness with which he communicates his instructions to the others is a mystery. Understanding them is a matter of intuition, an intuition that begins to develop at the age of four or five years when a child is first placed in front of a loom.

Often, the Master himself sits with his fellow workers and knots his part of the carpet as he sings. Many of the masters know the pattern by heart. Legend tells of oustads who knew some 50—60 different carpet patterns with their exact color shades by heart, and also projected the same patterns on to different sizes.

There are six different phases of manufacture:

The production process

1. The warp is tightened around the upper and lower transversal beams of the loom. Seen from the side, these these threads form a succession of figure eights. They must be just sufficiently taut: if the thread snaps, it will be necessary to start the whole thing over again with a new thread. If a torn warp thread is knotted together, there will be small white burls in the pile.

2. A smooth strip of about 1 inch is woven straight across the lower end, where the carpet starts to be knotted. This is to give a purchase for the knots which start from the bottom upwards.

3. A row of the dyed woollen yarn is knotted in, i.e. the *pile* according to the design.

4. After each row, a weft thread is inserted and beaten down with a comb of wood or iron. And so the procedure continues, row after row, until the carpet is of the intended length. If there are two weft threads, the second is plaited in a "wave" between the warp threads. The beating down of the weft is tremendously important, since it is in this way that the carpet becomes tightly woven! One can see carpets whose pile is completely worn down, but whose pattern is still perfectly clear. It is the weft threads that are holding what remains of the sometime pile — the loops around the warp — in a firm grip.

5. When the final weft threads have been inserted, phase 2 recurs. A smooth narrow band is woven on to the end now concluded, to prevent the knots there from slipping out and coming loose.

When the carpet is cut down from the loom, some 6—8 in of the warp is left at both ends, the *fringe*. This also serves as a sort of guarantee, since machine-made carpets have sewn-on fringes.

6. This is where the *carpet cutter* enters the picture. He is an artist whose only tools are sensitive fingertips and a pair of curved scissors. Squatting over the spread carpet, he cuts the pile precisely as long or short as is aesthetically and qualitatively most suitable for the carpet in question. He notices any unevennesses more with his fingers than with the eye. When he has put down his scissors, there remains only the *languettage,* i.e. to bind the selvage, wash away the collected dust and loose fibres of many months' work.

In the great majority of carpets, the warp and weft threads are of cotton. Woollen yarn, mostly home-spun, is used only in a few pla-

Warp and knots

Sehna or
Persian knot

Ghiordes or
Turkish knot

ces in Kurdistan, by the Beluchi in Khurasan, and certain nomad tribes around Shiraz. Cotton is the better of the two yarns for this purpose, the carpet lies more firmly and evenly on the floor; a warp of woollen yarn can make a carpet flimsy, particularly if it is loosely knotted. Also, some of the warp can shrink owing to humidity, distorting the carpet.

For the particularly high qualities, and naturally in the weaving of silk carpets, silk thread is used for both warp and weft. Such thread is strong, pliable, and permits an extremely large number of knots per square inch.

Two different types of knots are used in Persia, the *Sehna* or *Persian knot,* and the *Ghiordes* or *Turkish knot.* Both are knotted around two warp threads. The Sehna knot takes a whole turn around the one thread, half a turn around the other; the Ghiordes knot runs in a loop around both threads, as shown in the picture.

Turkish knots give a slightly more full-bodied consistency to the carpet. From your point of view, however, it makes no difference whatsoever which knots have been used: the experience of centuries has shown both to be equally durable.

There is a variant on these two types of knot, called the *jufti* knot. Juft means twins or "couple" in Persian. The weaver runs his knot around *four* warp threads instead of the usual two. You can see this with a magnifying glass on the front of the carpet, if you fold it in and look at the bottom of the pile. The use of such knots is mere cheating, to reduce the period of manufacture. The method is used only by the workshops producing for export. In the name of truthfulness, it must be admitted that such carpets can be extremely good and hardwearing, in spite of the lesser number of knots. But they are unworthy the high art of Persian carpet-weaving.

Some Suggestions and Advice

It is impossible to formulate any sort of standard rule by which to calculate the current price of carpets. The only way of finding out the current level of prices is to shop round. To see and note the types, sizes and quality of carpets, and then to compare prices in the different shops. If you have read the chapter on prices carefully, you will have no difficulty in judging the real value of a carpet.

The majority of laymen are convinced that thick carpets are much better than thin, since the former will "wear" better. This is an error encouraged by authors who write about expensive thick carpets in which you "sink up to your ankles". A carpet that you sink into must be awfully loosely knotted.

One of the most important maxims is that *thickness is no guarantee of quality*. If by quality you mean the durability of a carpet, it is certainly not a question of long-cut wool but of *closeness* of weave!

A Persian saying runs: "The thinner the carpet, the richer its owner". A thin carpet is made of very thin yarn. Since the number of knots is extremely high, the manufacture of such a carpet demands a vast amount of time and great skill, since the artists tend with a thin creation to delight in a wealth of ornamentation.

It is impossible to obtain patterns equally delicate from coarser yarn. They fill the same surface with fewer knots, and the period of manufacture is thus shorter. Even so, the carpet can be "closely woven"! The other practical maxim is that the *thickness of the yarn maximizes the number of knots*. This means that you cannot knot a carpet more closely than to a certain limit. When this limit is reached, the carpet is as good as it can be.

Owing to this limitation, there is a closeness ratio between carpets woven of yarn of different thicknesses. This can be expressed as follows: *The thickness of the yarn is in inverse proportion to the number of knots*. Or more simply: if a carpet were manufactured of yarn five times the normal thickness, the number of knots would be five times less. And vice versa.

It would thus be unreasonable to compare two carpets of different type but the same size on the basis of number of knots. A Nain, for instance, which has 320 knots per square inch with a *Shiraz* that has 130. When we compare the carpets with others of their respective types, we can find that the carpet with three hundred knots per square inch is only a third class Nain, while the Shiraz is primus inter pares!

The quality gradings given after the description of each type of carpet are intended to help you to judge independently any type of carpet whatsoever. If you are not offered satisfactory information on number of knots in the shop, do not hesitate to count them yourself. This is not only easy, it is also fun. For safety's sake, take with you a small ruler and a magnifying glass.

Place the ruler on the back of the carpet, and with the help of a needle or pencil count the knots one inch in the direction of the warp threads and one inch transversally along the weft. Multiply the two figures, and you have the number of knots per square inch. To take an example, the number of knots is 11 lengthwise and 12 across. $11 \times 12 = 132$, which is the number of knots per square inch.

These gradings are based on a study of countless carpets of each individual type. The number of knots as given is obviously approxi-

Counting the knots on the back of a carpet. The carpet shown is knotted with Turkish or Ghiordes knots. Note that when counting in the one direction (from the ruler downwards in the picture), a Turkish knot can easily be taken for two if you are not careful. This is because the Turkish knot is looped around two warp threads, as shown in the drawing on p. 43. A knot is marked in the ring to the right of the pencil.

mative. Minor irregularities in the knotting are also inevitable, but of no great importance.

All the photographs in this book are newly taken. They show carpets of the types still available in the trade. It would not have served the purpose of this book to present a succession of antique carpets, the likes of which are never seen in the shops. Extensive collections can be seen by those who are interested in a number of museums, particularly in London, Vienna, Paris, Istanbul and New York.

Finally, one last word of advice before you go hunting for a carpet. Beware of the many attractive "finds" that are so cheap as to seem almost a present! No firm gives away its quality carpets.

What you will get for your money is a cheap carpet, for which you will have paid the proper price. The yarn in such a loosely knotted "find" will probably be of dust-dry tanner's wool, stripped from dead sheep and colored with the cheapest of synthetic dyes, without the least trace of the Orient's breathtaking fantasy in its simple pattern. Such a carpet is no adornment in the home.

Pay a bit more, and buy a better carpet. It's worth it. It need not be of the very best quality. It makes absurdly little difference whether it will stand up to 180 years of daily use or only 123. But you can be sure that it will age with you, that it will transform your house or apartment into a home, giving it warmth and comfort.

Don't forget what I said in a previous chapter: Buying a carpet cheaply does not mean buying a cheap carpet!

Good hunting!

Oriental Carpets in Color, with Descriptions

Abadeh

ABADEH is about 96 miles north of Shiraz. The carpets manufactured in this town originally carried the "Seli Sultan" design, row after row of small vases of flowers. The few bright carpets, with their red bouquets in dark grey vases on an ivory ground, were attractive to Western taste. The great bulk of production, however, incorporated the peculiar color combination of tobacco-colored vases and flowers on a pale yellow-beige ground. These carpets were neither colorful nor elegant. Nor, in spite of their quality, did they attract much of a price in the bazaars.

The poor market for them forced the weavers to think again. From time immemorial, the Kashghai tribes have pitched their summer camp more or less outside the town's gates. The weavers of Abadeh quite simply borrowed one of the Kashghai's most typical patterns and knotted their carpets by it, only in the Abadeh manner using cotton yarn for both warp and weft. The crossing proved successful. They achieved the beauty of the nomad carpets, but with greater weight, stability and wear.

Both the wool and dyes are excellent. A few of the latter are synthetic. A warm, deep red color predominates.

While the older carpets seldom exceed 6ft 6in × 4ft 3in, the new products are manufactured to any size. Persian knots.

The quality gradings are as follows:

No. of knots per inch

	length	breadth	No. of knots per sq in
A	15	14	210
B	14	13	182
C	10	12	120

Example of an Abadeh carpet, showing the influence of the Kashghai pattern. Cf. the carpet on p. 82.

Afghan

AFGHAN CARPETS are the only ones whose price curve has not rocketed along with the other oriental carpets. This is due more to over-production than to a pattern unchanged within human memory. Almost 95 percent of all these carpets are patterned with large octagons known as "filpa" or "elephant feet".

Afghans were once regarded as typical "men's study" carpets, or something "genuine" to put under a dining-room table. Today, they are used anywhere a quiet carpet is suitable.

The color composition consists of a very warm ox-blood red with streaks of indigo blue and sometimes a few knots of the lamb's natural beige wool. This gives an attractively harmonic appearance. You will also find in the trade what we call "Golden Afghan". The majority of these carpets were originally red, and have been toned down to their golden color by a chemical process.

Afghans come in all conceivable sizes. Large carpets of up to 20 × 13ft are not uncommon. Most sold, however, are the dozars — c. 6ft 6in × 4ft — and the "Baby Afghans" c. 4ft × 2ft 9in — whether they have an "elephant foot" or prayer-niche pattern. Extremely interesting examples are to be found among the small carpets intended for camel bags, particularly those made by the Beshir tribe.

Since both warp and weft are of lamb's or goat's wool, the carpet is very soft. It needs a rubber or felt underlay, if it is not to slip or ruck. If kept in a very humid place or unprofessionally cleaned, the edges of the carpet can become wavy or one side shorter than the other, owing to uneven tensions in the yarn. If this happens, the carpet should be stretched. The carpet is dampened, the sides are pulled out to an even length and nailed fast to the floor. After a few days, the carpet will have regained its original shape. Some carpet firms and cleaners undertake work of this kind.

Older Afghans are still to be found in the trade. These have a rusty brown ground, and usually a broad kilim weave at both short ends. They attract considerably higher prices than the newer carpets, but then their quality is also much higher.

In Dowlatabad there is made a heavier, very evenly knotted carpet with a velour-like pile and Bukhara pattern. These cost some 50 percent more than the ordinary Afghans, and are well worth their price.

Afghan carpets with less common patterns are more valuable than those with "elephant feet".

The quality gradings are as follows:

No. of knots per inch

	length	breadth	No. of knots per sq in
A	9	9	81
B	8	7	56
C	7	6	42
Dowlatabad carpets			
A	13	9	117
B	11	8	88

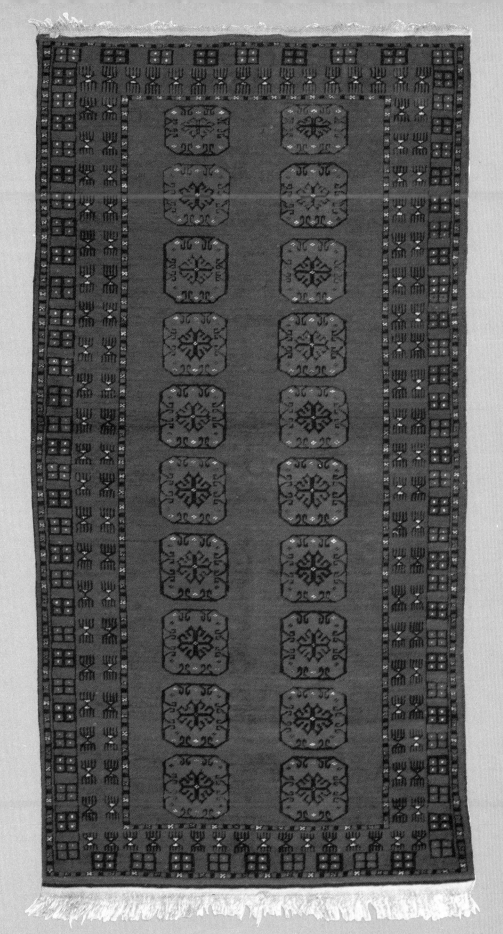

Afshar

AFSHAR is the name of a Persian nomadic tribe that was powerful in the 16th century, but subsequently split into two branches and lost its power and importance. The Kurdish tribe re-emerged briefly into the light of history two centuries later, when Nadir Shah sat upon the Peacock Throne that he had himself taken from India among the spoils of war. When he was murdered, the tribe declined once more into anonymity. Its carpets lost their specific character. They adopted the Kurdish style and patterning — they are of the tough, thick, heavy type — and are now called after the Kurdish villages in which they are made.

The other branch lives much further to the south, beyond Kirman. They use the same woollen yarn as in the Kirman carpets — soft, and with a great deal of animal fat in the fibres — and are also known as Kirman-Afshars. They have a very attractive lustre.

The pattern is always geometrical, usually consisting of one or two rhombs or a stepped cross enclosed in an elongated hexagon. Other popular patterns are cypresses, "Mir i botah" and the Tree of Life, the branches of which are depicted in straight lines. Many simplified versions of the neighbouring Kirman patterns also occur. The figures otherwise common among nomads, such as cocks, camels, people etc, are here rare.

Their coloring is tasteful, the main elements being dark blue sometimes merging into dark brown, an attractive pale red, and yellow-beige.

Large carpets are extremely rare. The usual size is c. 6ft × 4ft 6in, a fairly broad carpet in relation to its length, and a smaller version of about 5ft × 3ft 6in.

The warp and weft are of cotton. Turkish knots.

The quality gradings are as follows:

	No. of knots per inch		
	length	breadth	No. of knots per sq in
A	12	10	120
B	11	9	99

Ardebil

THE WORLD'S most famous carpet is called after this town in Azerbaijan, whose mosque it adorned before it became the pearl of the Victoria and Albert Museum's collection. Of the few 16th century carpets preserved, it is the only one to bear a date. The Moslem date — 1539 by our chronology — and the following humble lines are woven into the carpet:

"I have no retreat in the world other than to Thy threshold, my head has no other protection than this archway. The slave at this holy threshold, Makhsoud from Kashan, completed this work in 946".

The carpet's general type, its pattern and the Persian knots are as alien to Ardebil as was Makhsoud. He came from a town widely known for its weaving, some 500 miles to the South-East. Ardebil (or Ardabil) actually has no great past, no traditions to fall back on. The few carpets still to be found are neither technically nor artistically remarkable. With their symbol-free ornamentation, simple medallions and flowers, they remind us of the cheapest of Tabriz carpets. The warp and weft are of cotton.

The carpets produced in the past few decades differ essentially from the old carpets. The pattern is taken from the old Caucasian Shirvan carpets, which vanished from the European market with the creation of the USSR. Some sharp businessmen noticed that the buyers were combing the frontier districts for these Caucasians, and drew the conclusion that they were in great demand. They therefore decided to manufacture such carpets themselves.

What they achieved has nothing in common with its model apart from the pattern. Although they used wool for both the warp and weft, they failed to achieve the Caucasian character. The bright selvage along the sides is irritating, as are the unnecessarily long fringes. Few colors are used; a lively red and attractive midnight blue alternate with the widely displayed natural beige of the yarn.

Sizes vary from c. 4ft × 2ft 8in up to 9ft × 6ft, seldom larger.

Such a carpet is a good piece of handiwork, strong but soft. It requires a rubber underlay. It is also erroneously called a Shirvan in the trade. Its quality hardly varies. Turkish knots.

No. of knots per inch

	length	breadth	No. of knots per sq in
A	15	16	240
B	10	15	150
C	10	10	100

The Ardebil carpets most frequently found in the trade today have a pattern resembling that on the famous carpet in the Victoria and Albert Museum. This pattern is also common in many other districts.

Bakhtiari

THE BAKHTIARI are a Kurdish tribe who live partly as nomads, and who dwell in an area stretching from Isfahan to south of Malayer.

The tribe is as colorful as the carpets it manufactures. These are of rustic type, and good value for money. They are extremely hard-wearing, the wool and lively dyes are excellent. The strong warp and — usually blue — weft threads give these carpets weight, they lie firmly on the floor.

The best carpets are made by those of the tribe living in Chahar Mahal, near Isfahan. Since they are sold in the bazaars of Isfahan, they are known also as Isfahan-Bakhtiari. With more organized working conditions and access to larger looms, they have begun to make also larger carpets, up to 13ft × 10ft. The nomad carpets keep to the usual dozar sizes: c. 6ft 6in × 4ft 3in.

Those who are permanently settled display a greater variety of pattern, since — wittingly or unwittingly — they are greatly influenced by nearby Isfahan. Otherwise, what we mean by a "typical" Bakhtiari is a "garden carpet" with cypresses and peacocks in its panels. Another version is made up of pointed ellipses enclosed by non-parallel waves, with different patterns in each ellipse.

Purely illustrative carpets are extremely rare. This is not a bad thing, since the figures would seem clumsy owing to the heavy yarn employed.

The nomad Bakhtiari call their best carpets "Bibibaff", which means that they are made by the old ladies, their most experienced weavers.

The warp and weft threads are of cotton. The majority of the numerous dyes used are of vegetable origin. Persian knots.

The quality gradings are as follows:
No. of knots per inch

	length	breadth	No. of knots per sq in
A	13	12	156
B	10	10	100
C	9	8	72

Baluchi

THE BALUCHI are a people consisting of several tribes, some of whom are still nomads. Those who are permanently settled live in Baluchistan in eastern Persia and Afghanistan. In both countries, they weave carpets. The products of their Afghan cousins go under the name of "Baluchi". Known in the trade as "Herat-Baluchi", they are cheap, losely knotted, and sloppy. We shall not concern ourselves with them here.

The carpets made in Persia are called "Meshed-Baluchi" after the capital of Khurasan, in whose bazaars they are sold. These carpets are usually of high quality. Their sober elegance surprises us, it is difficult to believe that a nomad people can achieve such tasteful carpets.

The colors used are few, a deep warm red and indigo blue in several different shades, occasionally with a few natural knots. The effect is one of unrivalled harmony.

A wealth of variations on the basic pattern occur, and almost every family has its own. The ornamentation is strictly geometrical. The niches on the prayer carpets are neither pointed like those of the Turks, nor roundly arched like those of the Persians, but proceed in straight lines at angles of 90 degrees. The prayer carpets often have a central field the color of camelhair, and a Tree of Life with horizontal branches. The occasional carpet also has a hand with extended fingers in the upper corners.

Countless ornamental designs are employed, and an attempt is made to get them symmetrical. In the border, you often see the Running Dog, a softer version of the meander. Birds and horses are now sometimes woven into the carpets, but they are as yet fairly rare.

Formats are of nomad type, from c. 7ft × 4ft downwards. Usually fairly small. Gallery (runner) or Extra Large carpets are unusual. On the other hand, there are some delightful small donkey bags.

The older carpets are of considerably greater value. They are dyed with guaranteed genuine vegetable colors. The indigo shines in the loveliest shades of midnight blue. They usually have kilim weaves at the ends, the sides being artistically plaited.

The yarn is excellent, spun from the lustrous sheep's wool of Meshed, i.e. of Khurasan. The warp and weft threads are also of wool, recently also of cotton. Persian knots.

The quality gradings are as follows:
No. of knots per inch

	length	breadth	No. of knots per sq in
A	10	15	150
B	8	13	104
C	8	8	64

Bijar

A SMALL TOWN populated by Kurds has given its name to what is easily the heaviest and — in relation to the thickness of its yarn — the closest woven of all Persian carpets. The skill and strength deployed by the weavers in beating down the rows of knots until the carpet is compact as an oak plank excites admiration. Nor does one see a Bijar carpet, however old, that has become worn by normal use.

Patterns are symmetrical, whether the cental field is filled with ornamentation or consists of a monochrome panel. One of the more frequent designs is the "Herati" pattern, on a dullish wine-red or dark-blue ground. Also typical is the Kurdish "anchor medallion" — ending in anchors instead of the usual arrowheads. Other carpets have a medallion consisting of an up-ended square. "Gül Franghin", French roses or the Louis Philippe pattern, were made to the order of French customers in the mid 1840's. The pattern survived the French monarchy by over a century, and is still in use.

We have already mentioned the main colors. The complementary colors are also in dullish shades, apart from a bright celestial blue. A color used only in Bijars is "malva", or mauve.

The wool is from mountain sheep, tough and strong. The warp and weft threads can be of wool — sometimes mixed with goat's wool — and cotton. Turkish knots.

Large carpets used to be popular for their ability to withstand heavy furniture. The shortage of domestic help and the decreasing size of residences have reduced the demand — these carpets weigh nearly 1 lb per sq ft. The most common size is now the dozar — c. 6ft 6in × 4ft 3in — and other sizes are made only on a very small scale.

These carpets should be rolled. If folded, the warp and weft threads can break. If you have to fold it, do so with the pile outwards.

Careless packaging has often caused damage. Before deciding for a Bijar, look at its back, particularly in the intersections of any folds, where the carpet may have broken. Minor damage is easy to sew together. Provided the repair is properly done, the damage will not be visible and neither the lifetime nor the value of the carpet will be affected. Larger repairs, particularly if they are visible on the front, will reduce the value.

The quality gradings are as follows:

No. of knots per inch

	length	breadth	No. of knots per sq in
A	14	14	196
B	10	10	100
C	8	8	64

Borchalou

BORCHALOU is a small district of only a couple of dozen villages, situated east of Hamadan. The carpets woven there are the only products in the great Hamadan area to display the curvilinear patterns of the more cultivated carpets. Round medallions instead of rhombs and squares, graceful designs rather than stiff, angular ornamentation. The broad "guard bands" with their flower motifs make an attractive framework to the field.

No great differences in quality are to be found among Borchalou carpets. They are almost all equally well knotted from lustrous, very hardwearing wool. The only possible criticism is their generous use of orange, turquoise, pink and yellow, colors greatly beloved by the Orient, which can give an agitated appearance to carpets with a bright ground.

The most common sizes are c. 6ft 6in × 5ft — fairly broad in relation to their lenght — and c. 5ft × 3ft 3in and 2ft 8in × 1ft 8in. Larger carpets are woven only on a small scale.

The warp and weft threads are of cotton. Turkish knots.

The quality gradings are as follows:

	No. of knots per inch		No. of knots per sq in
	length	breadth	
A	10	12	120
B	8	11	88

Bukhara

BUKHARA (Bokhara) is in the Soviet Republic of Turkmenistan. In the actual town, whose market was once greatly frequented by the caravans, no carpets at all are made. But the town has lent its name to the carpets of the Turkmen nomads, with their special patterns: shallow octagons repeated in rows over the entire surface. It was in the bazaars of Bukhara that the Turkmens sold the carpets woven by the women out on the steppes while the sheep were grazing.

Even today, the best carpets are manufactured by the Turkmen tribe living in Russia. These are thin, very evenly knotted, and have two distinguishing shades of color: on the slightly older carpets rusty brown, and on newer carpets streaks of Cardinal red. For nomad carpets, they have a very elegant and cultured appearance indeed.

These are closely followed by the Yomuds, the branch of the tribe living in Persia. If they fail to surpass their Russian cousins in quality, they do so in their fantasy. Their camel bags and tent hangings display numerous playful variations of pattern. Apart from the octagons — known as "gül", or rose pattern — they also display barbed rhombs or bars. The borders are as fine as on the Russian carpets, but the short end is extended by an extra border, a sort of tribal mark that can consist of bent combs, crabs, and other objects difficult to identify.

The tent hanging or "hatchlin" is called in the native slang "purdah" — the veil with which the women cover their faces. Such a hanging has a character all its own, with a quartered central field without any octagons, and an extremely assymmetrical border. The most characteristic ornamental designs are spurs in the central field, and zigzag lines in the border.

Bukhara carpets are also made in Afghanistan. These are thicker and heavier, with a velour-like surface and the warm red color of Afghan carpets. They are regarded in the trade as high-quality Afghans, and referred to as Dowlatabads from the town in which they are made. Cf. p. 50.

The "P. Bukhara" or "Pak Bukhara" carpets displayed in many shops are from Pakistan. They have nothing whatsoever to do with the Turkmen carpets. See further under "Pakistani carpets", p. 129.

The warp and weft threads in Bukhara are of woollen yarn — previously always home-spun — and with unnecessarily long fringes. Turkish knots.

The quality gradings for Russian Bukharas are as follows:

	No. of knots per inch		
	length	breadth	No. of knots per sq in
A	20	18	360
B	18	16	288
C	17	12	204
For Yomud Bukharas:			
A	19	14	266
B	18	12	216
C	16	8	128

Feraghan

UNTIL WORLD WAR I, carpets from the Feraghan district south-east of Teheran enjoyed enormous popularity in the West. Their name became synonymous with the "Herati" pattern — the town had practically sole rights to the classical design of a rhomb surrounded by four small fishes. The English called this the "gentleman's carpet", by reason of its sober elegance. It had either indigo blue or the same rusty red ground as was otherwise boasted only by the Malayer and early Saruk carpets.

The demand was great, and Persian homes began to be emptied of their treasures. The buyers offered such high prices that not even the wealthiest Persians could resist. Fortunately, there was a very large reserve to draw on. It is still possible to find the occasional older carpet in the shops.

The years between the wars saw a period of decline, and the bottom was reached soon after World War II. Since then, only a few carpets of the old standard have been cut down from the looms. Most of the weavers went over to other sorts of carpet, mainly Saruks. They work on contract for the big exporters, who pay them by the week as work proceeds.

Since the "Herati" pattern does not have the same effect on coarsely knotted carpets, some of the weavers borrowed simpler patterns from the villages around Hamadan. These carpets are quicker to make, and give quicker money. It is entirely wrong to call these Feraghan carpets. Their wool is not as fine as in a true Feraghan, nor are the dyes used of vegetable origin.

The format of the older carpets was either the dozar — c. 6ft 6in × 4ft 3in — or the kellegi — c. 16ft 6in × 6ft 6in, 13ft × 5ft 6in (like the long narrow carpets, but they don't keep to the Gallery, or runner, format); the new Feraghans keep to the dozar size.

Warp and weft threads of cotton. Turkish knots.

The quality gradings are as follows:

	No. of knots per inch		No. of knots per sq in
	length	breadth	
A	12	12	144
B	10	10	100

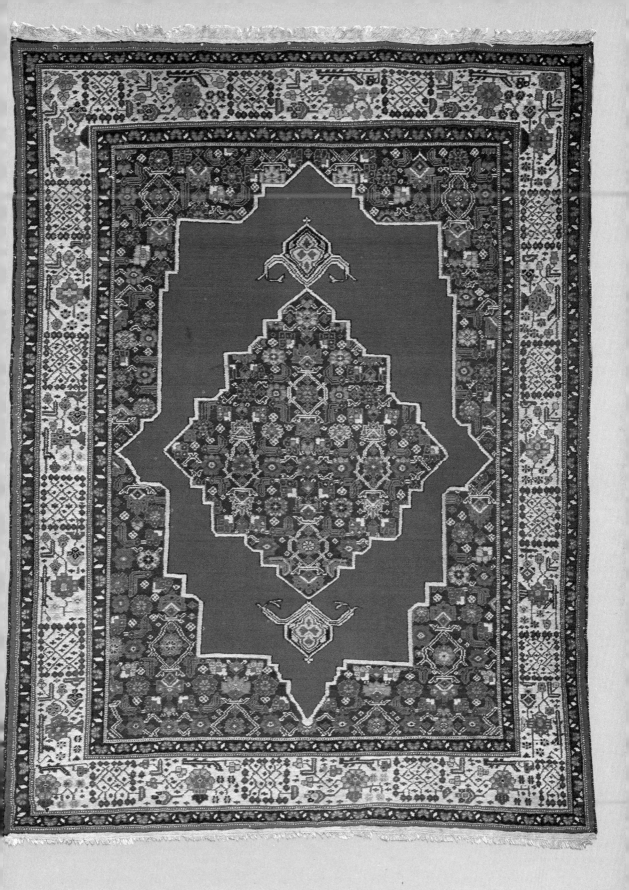

Hamadan

HAMADAN is one of the oldest cities in the world. As Ekbatana, it was once the capital of the Medes. Here ruled Ahasueros, of the Book of Esther, whose queen Esther became. The city is some 70 miles south-west of Teheran, in one of the greatest carpet-producing areas in all Persia. The carpets actually made in the city comprise only a fraction of those sold in Hamadan's bazaars. The rest come from the hundreds of villages scattered around Hamadan.

The carpets described as Hamadans differ widely in pattern, their common denominator being a special method of knotting. While the rest of Persia uses a double weft thread after each knotted row, this district has only one. The double weft threads loop around the warp and hide it from sight, while the single weft thread covers only half. On the back of a Hamadan, every warp thread can thus be seen as a broken line.

Another characteristic of these carpets is their heaviness. They have a great deal of wool in the pile, and a thick cotton warp. Their patterns seem simple by comparison with other Persian carpets, since the ornamentation is coarser. The variations are infinite. Difficult-to-interpret or distorted motifs and ornamental designs are mixed with ancient symbols whose meaning has been forgotten for generations. Imaginative medallions, tortoise and other patterns are mixed with pictures of people, rams, camels, cocks or birds, as primitively portrayed as in children's drawings.

Extremely interesting examples are still to be found among the slightly older carpets. However, the most attractive finds are to be made among the Gallery carpets, which have best preserved their original oriental character.

The carpets made in Hamadan itself are of high quality. They are of strong, thick and heavy structure, like the Saruks. They are known either as Shahrbaff — knotted in the city — or Kazvin, after the weavers from Kazvin who have settled there. The number of knots is about 160 per sq in.

The formats most frequent in the Hamadan area are the dozar, c. 6ft 6in × 4ft 3in, zaronim, c. 5ft × 3ft 3in, zarcharak, c. 4ft × 2ft 8in, and poshti in sizes of about 2ft 8in × 2ft, plus Gallery (runner) carpets. Large carpets are rare.

One also sees in the trade a very cheap carpet, some 6ft 6in × 3ft 3in in size, that is sometimes sold under the name of Hamadan, Tachtekabi, Canapé, Mossul or Barik. This is a sub-standard product made entirely to attract customers. Its wool is dry and dead, its dyes poor, and the number of knots far too small, c. 40 knots per sq in. It can become worn in places after only a year or so.

The warp and weft threads of Hamadans are of cotton. Turkish knots.

The quality gradings are as follows:

| | No. of knots per inch | | |
	length	breadth	No. of knots per sq in
A	8	10	80
B	7	9	63
C	6	8	48

Haroon

HAROON or Haruni is a name to remember. In this little village, about 40 miles south-west of Isfahan, a small number of carpets are woven whose pattern is amazingly like the qualitatively far superior Kashans. The less knowledgeable sellers refer to them erroneously as Haruni-Kashans, thus lending the lustre of the Kashan name to the much cheaper Haroons.

If the carpet's origin is not betrayed by the pattern, it will be by the dyes and wool. The yarn is dry and lustreless, in strong contrast to the velvety surface of a Kashan. Nor does the range of colors fit. The orange-yellow colors so popular in the Orient are generously displayed. Even the red shows a touch of orange. This you never see on a good Kashan. If a few carpets of really high quality are achieved, they are usually overpatterned, almost blurred. Most successful are the prayer carpets with a "mihrab", or prayer-niche pattern.

The wool can vary considerably, but is seldom of the highest quality. The same applies to the dyes. Warp and weft of cotton. Persian knots.

The quality gradings are as follows:

No. of knots per inch

	length	breadth	No. of knots per sq in
A	14	17	238
B	12	13	156
C	9	12	108

Heriz

HERIZ is in Azerbaijan, where they make the largest carpets in all Persia. Heriz is the best known of the three dozen villages in the district. Its carpets are far superior to the others in quality. The silk carpets woven until World War I surpass everything. It is difficult to find the equal of these smooth, thin silken carpets — which were woven in sizes of up to 29 square yards! They appear only occasionally when a collector dies, and his estate goes under the hammer. The big woollen carpets from this period are also rarities. They appear occasionally in the trade, although they attract very high prices.

The new Heriz is made of coarser yarn, so that the number of knots is fairly low. This is of little importance as regards wear. In highly exposed places such as hotel vestibules, they have proved highly resistent to wear, demonstrating the excellence of the material and skill of the weavers. Particularly fine carpets are called in the bazaars Peshm-i-Meshed (=the wool is from Meshed).

The patterns used are few, the most popular and characteristic being the medallion pattern with acanthus leaves and palmettes in the field, and attractive corner pieces.

Formats are limited downwards, but upwards there seems almost no limit: 26ft × 19ft 6in and even larger sizes are not at all uncommon.

The colors are discreet. The red color is very deep. Blue occurs in several shades, from indigo to a very attractive bright blue. The corners or central fields are usually of ivory beige.

Warp and weft of cotton. Turkish knots.

The quality gradings are as follows:

No. of knots per inch

	length	breadth	No. of knots per sq in
A	10	8	80
B	9	6	54

Ingelas

INGELAS is a small town 6 miles outside Hamadan. It is known for good carpets at a relatively low price.

These carpets have only one pattern, The Herati. This travels from border to border, without variation. Never an improvised detail, only rarely a medallion.

The wool is of good quality, as are the few dyes used. The ground is dark red, complemented by dark blue — or vice versa. The third color is usually the undyed natural beige wool, usually in the border or a few knots here and there.

Ingelas is a compact, extremely durable carpet. The most usual format is about 6ft 10in × 4ft 9in, somewhat broader than dozars in general. Smaller carpets exist, but these are as rare as the Gallery carpets. Warp and weft of cotton. Turkish knots. The quality is very even, and only one grading is given from which to make comparisons.

No. of knots per inch

length	breadth	No. of knots per sq in
10	9	90

Isfahan

THE ISFAHAN carpet's family tree dates back to the late 16th century, when the Persian sun-king Shah Abbas built up the town to be his new capital. Isfahan, which soon became larger than Elizabethan London, had an enormous need of carpets. The grand palaces, the mosques, all the new buildings demanded carpets.

A court carpet-weaving shop was set up. Artists and élite weavers were recruited from all parts of the Great Persian Empire. Some of the best craftsmen actually returned from the workshops of the Grand Moguls. For centuries to come, the achievements of this select band provided an inexhaustible source of inspiration for later generations.

New patterns and ornamental designs were composed, all with a perfect rythm and ingenious balance. The medallions resembled mounted jewels. Dynamic scenes of battle alternated with fables and legendary figures. 500 Chinese, who in the absence of kaolin failed to produce porcelain for the Shah, left behind them some graceful designs. The weavers returning from India contributed new prayer niches, new variations of color and pattern. The forgotten art of weaving gold and silver threads into silk carpets was revived. Magnificent showpiece carpets were created.

The court workshop was closed in the early 18th century, when the town was occupied by the Afghans. Only after World War I did Isfahan carpets appear once more on the European markets. They were entirely worthy of their predecessors, and are still among the most outstanding of oriental carpets. They are thin, and closely woven. The pile is cut down to a few millimetres, the contours of the pattern emerge with extreme clearness.

Almost all these carpets have a bright ground, and symmetrical design. The medallions are round, adorned with 8 or 16 points. Only about 5 percent of production consists of carpets with illustrative motifs: birds, The Tree of Life, vases, animals and prayer niches are the most popular patterns. The coloring is sober, even the feathers of the birds being discreetly toned down.

The most common size is c. 6ft 10in × 4ft 3in. Large carpets of high quality are woven in very limited numbers. Such a carpet can take several years to make, and the price is accordingly high. The prayer carpets, 5ft × 3ft 3in, are also rare.

However, larger carpets are also produced in a simpler manner, originally for the Arab countries. These are now exported also to the West. They are woven with "jufti" knots; the number of knots is less, and the pattern less finely chiselled. The woollen yarn and dyes are also of a lower quality.

The wrap and weft threads are of cotton, or in the very best carpets of silk. Persian knots.

The quality gradings are as follows:

No. of knots per inch

	length	breadth	No. of knots per	
A	28	24	672	sq in
B	23	20	460	
C	18	17	306	
New Arabian Isfahan:				
	15	16	240	

Karadja

KARADJA or Karaja comprises a handful of villages in Azerbaijan, some 35 miles northeast of Tabriz. The district is best known for its Gallery carpets.

Until World War II, Karadja produced a limited number of carpets of decent quality. Since the 1950's, production has increased as quality has fallen. Karadja carpets became a widely demanded staple commodity in the lower price range. The unusually thick yarn, which means a lesser number of knots, meant that they could be produced more quickly and cheaply. Since the rows of knots are properly beaten down, the carpets seem closely woven, stiff and hard-wearing. In combination with the low price, the erroneous view that thick carpets are best has made them very easy to sell.

Their most characteristic feature is the pattern, the same on all Karadja carpets. This consists of geometrical medallions, the number of which depends on the carpet's length. The border, on the other hand, can vary slightly: it consists, usually, of garland designs that have been borrowed from the Tabriz carpets, and altered out of recognition by the straight lines.

The colors are synthetic, and indeterminate. It is impossible to quote any particular color composition.

The Gallery (runner) carpets can be very long, but the greatest demand is for the shortest and most narrow. A lesser number of dozar sizes are produced, c. 6ft × 4ft 6in, and a very large number of poshti, c. 2ft 8in × 2ft, these too with exactly the same pattern. Few large carpets are made, however.

The warp and weft threads are of cotton and are also of coarse quality. Turkish knots.

The quality gradings are as follows:

No. of knots per inch

	length	breadth	No. of knots per sq in
A	10	7	70
B	8	6	48

Kashan

KASHAN was famous for its brocades even in the Middle Ages, but the chronicles say nothing of its carpets. It is claimed that the pearl of the Victoria and Albert collection, the "Ardebil" carpet dated to 1539, should properly be classified as a Kashan, since it was made according to the inscription by one Makhsoud from Kashan. It is impossible, however, to point to any antique carpet that was demonstrably made in Kashan.

The first organized production of carpets in Kashan was started in the late 19th century by the famous weavers Mouchtashemi, Yakoutiel and Mullah Ismael, whose carpets attract higher prices in Persia than in the West. Since this time, Kashans have held a distinguished position on the world market.

Their success has been due to three factors: the richly variable pattern and attractive colors; the soft, lustrous Merino wool that gives these carpets their velvety surface; and the masterly skill of the weavers engaged from nearby Isfahan. All this resulted in a cultivated oriental carpet, with a Western elegance.

The most important of the innumerable variations in pattern are as follows: 1. The classical pattern, with a long medallion and corner decoration. The field is rich in flowers, vines, arabesques and palmettes of the Shah Abbas type, but never symbols of any kind. 2. The prayer carpets with the "mihrab" or prayer niche, with Persian, Assyrian or Corinthian pillars supporting the arch, and a hanging lamp over the monochrome field. 3. A livelier version of the ancient vase pattern. The bouquets resemble a display of peacock feathers. 4. The illustrative carpets, the usual composition of which comprises a mass of small birds among flowers and branches. Least in demand are the overdimensioned figures, usually swarthy old men of dismal countenance.

The border is worth particular mention. It is always beautiful, whether purely ornamental, consisting of figures, or with inscriptions in cartouches. Inscriptions increase the value of the carpet.

Both the Merino wool and the local product, which is also used, are outstanding. The carpets woven from Merino wool are termed "Kurk Kashan" and attract a higher price.

The dyes are first-class, even the synthetic ones. The majority of carpets have a warm red ground, the rest are indigo. Occasionally beige or some other color.

The silk carpets deserve a chapter to themselves. While the other towns, apart from Qum, have completely stopped making them, Kashan continues the tradition. "Part silk" carpets are also made. In these, part of the pattern is knotted in silk yarn to enhance the effect. Silk carpets incorporating gold or silver threads are rarities. Their closeness of weave is usually around 420—450 knots per sq in.

The warp and weft threads of the "normal" Kashans are of cotton. Persian knots.

The quality gradings are as follows:

No. of knots per inch

	length	breadth	No. of knots per sq in
A	. 20	20	400
B	18	18	324
C	15	15	225
D	11	11	121

See plates overleaf

Kashghai

THE KASHGHAI are the most powerful of all Persia's nomad tribes. Their area extends from Isfahan down towards Shiraz. They are a proud, freedom-loving people, whose black goatskin tents house a wealth of portraits of shot rebel ancestors. The men have a reputation as outstanding horsemen, the women as great carpet-weavers.

The carpets are the tribe's own product from beginning to end. The Kashghai spin yarn from the wool cut from their own sheep, and color it according to their own recipes with dyes made from plants picked around the camp.

The numerous different patterns are also their own. The women weave them from memory. As with all nomad carpets, the patterns are geometrical, mainly with one to three rhombs in the field. A characteristic feature is their richness of detail. The weavers often improvise, deviate from the family's traditional pattern and put in the occasional odd figure. The drawings are naive, mostly of birds, animals, horsemen, and trees — the living environment of the camp. Or stars, symbols and various small ornaments that recall the Caucasian carpets. The Kashghai came from the Caucasus four centuries ago.

The borders are always tasteful and imaginative, displaying infinite variety: finely patterned bands, oblique streaks, stepped motifs, garlands and stars.

Truly illustrated carpets are rare, typical, however, is the three-trunked Tree of Life, a Trinitarian symbol of heathen origin.

The older, finer and smaller carpets are also termed "Mecca Shiraz". These were originally sold in the bazaars of Shiraz, and pilgrims used to take them to Mecca as prayer carpets.

Both warp and weft are of wool. The warp is often dark, since it is usually of goat-hair. The wool is soft and has a great deal of animal fat in the fibres, giving the carpets an attractive

lustre. As already mentioned, the dyes are vegetable. The shade most appreciated by the Persians themselves is a subdued rusty red. Older carpets in this color are in great demand.

The most frequent sizes are c. 6 × 4ft and 5ft × 3ft 3in. The Kashghai also make very attractive saddle cloths, and camel and donkey bags.

The quality gradings are as follows:

No. of knots per inch

	length	breadth	No. of knots per sq in
A	11	13	143
B	8	10	80
C	6	5	30

Kelardasht

KELARDASHT is an obscure little village by the Caspian Sea. The name is not worth remembering, unless you are a carpet-lover. Only a few carpets come from Kelardasht, but what wonderful carpets they are! Carpets such as lay beneath the feet of madonnas and popes, or are to be seen hanging from the balconies of the Doge's palace in Renaissance paintings.

These carpets are not displayed in shop windows, but lie rolled-up and forgotten in some dark corner of a back room. They are produced only if the carpet dealer senses that he is dealing with a "Liebhaber".

There is a reason for their rarity. Kelardasht is the only place in the world of Islam where a woman is permitted to keep the household's carpets if her husband puts her away. He'll keep her, rather than lose these splendid carpets.

And yet the carpets of Kelardasht cannot compete qualitatively, in number of knots, with the "big names". The hand-spun, coarsely fibred goat-hair yarn used in the warp has never been twined so thinly as to permit any very large number of knots per square inch.

The pattern is classical: shallow, elegant octagons around barbed polygons in different colors, all on an attractive deep-red field. In the main border, it is customary to find four arrow-heads pointed against each other; in the narrow guard bands, a crenellated design.

The above applies to the somewhat older carpets, between 30 and 60 years old.

In the mid 1960's, a number of exporters encouraged the people of the village to weave carpets for them. These appear occasionally on the market, but are nowhere near as attractive as the carpets they make for themselves.

The yarn is colored with vegetable dyes. The wool is excellent, with a natural lustre. The warp and weft are of goat-hair, less frequently of cotton. Turkish knots.

Sizes are usually small, 6 × 4ft, or else Gallery or kellegi format: 9ft 3in × 3ft 3in or 11ft 6in × 4ft 6in, or thereabouts. The Gallery (runner) carpets are those most in demand.

The quality gradings are as follows:

No. of knots per inch

	length	breadth	No. of knots per sq in
A	9	11	99
B	8	10	80
C	7	9	63

Qum

Qum (or Khum), 90 miles south of Teheran, is Persia's second most holy city, where Mohammed's daughter Fatima lies buried among kings and peasantry.

No carpet-making on a large scale took place there until the 30's. Since then experiments have been made with different patterns. Early Sehna, Kashan, Isfahan and other better quality carpets were copied in various combinations. The border from one carpet would be combined with the field of another, certain ornamental designs replaced by others. In this way quite a lot of new patterns were obtained, but these carpets were long lacking in originality. A characteristic feature, however, was an ivory beige ground, and frequent use of the light green colour that is otherwise so rare on Persian carpets. A new generation of artists have now taken over the design, and several new patterns have been created; above all in an attractive turquoise colour combination, these have given the carpets from Qum a new profile.

Among the many patterns, four in particular have enjoyed great success on the world market. The *garden design,* in which the field is divided into small squares like flowerbeds, containing different flower motifs and figures. The *striped design,* consisting exclusively of stripes in different colors and ornamentation running with the length of the carpet. The great throne-room in the Golestan Palace in Teheran is covered with striped carpets of this kind, of varying provenance and 70 – 80 square yards in size. The *illustrative* carpets can depict birds, winged lions, dragons, old Persian hunting scenes, historical scenes, etc. etc. In this respect, the imagination of the artists seems inexhaustible. The birds and animals are usually of silk yarn. The *prayer niche* is also common.

These carpets are evenly knotted, with a short-cut pile, and they are very hard-wearing. The only objection one might make is that they are excessively sober, and show no trace of improvisation. The strict control under which they are manufactured allows no deviation. The same applies to the silk carpets, which predominantly carry the popular hunting motif.

Sizes range from c. 6ft 10in × 4ft 3in up to c. 9ft 9in × 13ft. No overdimensioned carpets that will be difficult to sell, or unprofitable little squares: production is geared to exports.

The warp and weft are of cotton. Turkish knots.

The quality gradings are as follows:

No. of knots per inch

	length	breadth	No. of knots per sq in
A	16	17	272
B	13	15	195
C	11	13	143

Kirman

KIRMAN carpets or Kerman carpets as they should properly be called after the Southern Persian city in which they are made, have topped the popularity charts for Persian carpets for decades. Their success is due to their constituting a richer variant of the Aubusson pattern. Glowing colors instead of anaemic, cascades of flowers instead of garlands and medallions consisting of only a few flowers.

Kerman was not subject to the same commercial stimulus as other towns with a more favorable position. It lay some months by caravan from the contemporary trade centres of Constantinople and Tabriz, and its small-scale carpet production was not thought important enough to warrant a visit. Early this century, when the town began to be discovered by foreign buyers, there were only a few carpets available, but these all the more magnificent. Their manufacture was soon organized, and the production curve rocketed.

During the time that followed, the makers luxuriated in the composition of new patterns. The shawl pattern, large "Mir i botah" drawn with points and resembling an enormous filigree work. The panel pattern, a sort of garden pattern with panels decorated in various ways and inscriptions along the pathways between the "flowerbeds". "Ashraf — Bid i majnun", moon-daisies and weeping willows that give an harmonic impression in spite of the overpatterning. The "Mihrab" carpet, with a prayer niche showing an Indian influence, and a field filled with vases, flowers and sometimes a Tree of Life. "Shekarghan" — a hunting theme, which is otherwise rare on long-cut carpets. "Möborak boshad" — wedding carpets with inwoven best wishes for the newly married couple, and ordered perhaps by the bride's parents while she was still in the cradle.

Not until the 30's was the most successful carpet of all produced. This has a border chock full of flowers, and an oblong medallion consisting entirely of roses. It was from this that the "Chubkoranin" later developed, the Koran cover pattern with a large monochrome panel and more strictly limited border, but as filled with roses as its predecessor.

The wool around Kerman is outstanding, with an extremely high fat content. This gives the carpets a very bright lustre. The pile is cut half-long. The warp and weft are of cotton. Turkish knots. The dyes are for the most part synthetic, but of high quality.

The prices of Kerman carpets have kept pace with the cost of living in Iran. To meet the demand of customers for cheaper products, carpets are also made with a simplified pattern, far fewer knots, dryer wool yarn and inferior dyes. I would advise most strongly against buying these losely knotted — less than 90 knots per sq in — sub-standard products.

The quality gradings are as follows:

No. of knots per inch

	length	breadth	No. of knots per sq in
A	16	18	288
B	12	15	180
C	11	12	132

Lilihan

LILIHAN is the centermost of some half dozen villages in the district of Kemereh, south of Arak. The area is populated by Armenians, famous carpet-weavers in their own country, who were forcibly transported there in the 17th century.

The people of these villages weave a unique sort of carpet, called after the largest village, Lilihan. These carpets are characterized by an unusual pink shade, and a pattern unlike anything woven elsewhere. The medallion is drowned in flowers, leaves and ornamental designs like fans or cloud ribbons, the whole surface being strewn with them. The interesting thing is that the medallions almost always conceal a cross. The illustration will explain the pattern better than the most exhaustive description.

Any deviations in pattern are extremely minor, which is a pity. These carpets are excellent, hard-wearing, comparatively thin and with a silky lustre.

The intermediate sizes are remarkable. They are unusually broad, about 5ft 3in to a length of 6ft 6in. The other carpets are more usual: 5ft × 3ft 3in, and in smaller quantities 9ft 9in × 6ft 6in. Plus a specifically oriental measurement: 9ft 9in × 5ft 3in.

The dyes are extremely good, usually of vegetable origin. Warp and weft of cotton. Turkish knots.

The quality gradings are as follows:

No. of knots per inch

	length	breadth	No. of knots per sq in
A	11	9	99
B	10	8	80
C	9	7	63

Malayer

MALAYER is a happy little town between Hamadan and Arak. The finest of grapes grow in its surroundings, and the area's most interesting carpets are woven here. Those who spoil themselves prefer Malayer carpets for their homes, even if they are technically and qualitatively inferior to the "big names". The reason is that they are so genuinely spontaneous, without a trace of alien influence. They are created, not manufactured. They seem to have been woven for the maker's own home, not to be sold.

The remarkable thing is that every Malayer looks different. Each family has a few of their own patterns, from which they weave. They can be symmetrical or assymmetrical, floral or geometrical, anything. The weavers also like to incorporate small figures. These are playfully simple, seemingly improvised, but there is still a fine balance of composition. For the most part, they are human figures, horsemen, camels, horses and pools with ducks and goldfish — the wealthy home's symbol of happiness. Since the carpets are much thinner than others from the same district, the pattern emerges more clearly.

The wool is excellent, with a natural lustre.

The dyes are usually organic, but synthetic dyes have begun to appear in the latest carpets. It is the rusty red, mixed with orange, that gives the carpet its special character. This color is effectively offset by the midnight-blue indigo. The natural beige of the wool softens up the impression, and bridges the contrasting colours. Only the earlier Feraghans and Saruks have a rusty red similar to the Malayer, and this is a help in identification.

Apart from the dozar sizes — c. 6ft 6in × 4ft 3in — the long kellegi is the most frequent format; a small number of zaronim, c. 5ft × 3ft 3in, are also made. Carpets larger than 9ft 3in × 5ft 3in are rare. With a bit of luck, you can find some splendid examples of these carpets in the trade at a reasonable price. People in the bazaar often put in one or two as bait in their "mixed" bales, and these can slip through unnoticed right up to the private buyer.

Warp and weft of cotton. Turkish knots.

The quality gradings are as follows:

	No. of knots per inch		
	length	breadth	No. of knots per sq in
A	10	10	100
B	8	9	72

Maslaghan

MASLAGHAN is a small district in the Saveh area. In the trade, the name implies a carpet that carries a "lightning pattern" and is manufactured in the single village of Kerdar.

Just as two drops of water are alike and yet unlike, so with the Maslaghans. They differ from each other only in small details. Some have tortoises in the border, others stars, scorpions or a stepped design. The field can be decorated with "Mir i botah", arrow-heads, moon-daisies or nothing at all. No figures are to be found, nor any dates.

The coloring is of great importance in price-setting. Particularly successful color combinations can practically double the price. The majority of carpets, however, have a clear red field.

Production at Kerdar has deteriorated since the mid 50's. Subsequent carpets are loosely knotted and the material is sub-standard, a typical clearance sale product.

The most common sizes are c. 6ft 6in × 4ft3in. Large carpets with the lightning pattern are unknown. Occasional kellegi are manufactured, c. 4ft 6in × 8ft 6in, and some zaronim of about 5ft × 3ft 3in.

Warp and weft of cotton. Turkish knots.

The quality gradings are as follows:

No. of knots per inch

	length	breadth	No. of knots per sq in
A	9	10	90
B	8	8	64
C	7	6	42

Mehraban

MEHRABAN is in Azerbaijan, 9 miles south of Heriz. The town and the villages around it were known for manufacturing only large carpets, and at very moderate prices. Carpets of 20 × 13ft are sold for less than what a mediocre Isfahan of 6ft 6in × 4ft 6in can cost. Obviously, you can't ask very much of such carpets. At the auctions, you often see Mehrabans about 30 years old that are if not completely worn out are at least very patchy.

The wool yarn is of low quality and very thick, as are the cotton warp and weft threads. The dyes are synthetic.

The patterns are imitations of those used in Tabriz, but they can be recognized only with difficulty. The coarse yarn prevents a curvilinear design, the lines are straight and angled.

Carpets like those of Mehraban are also made at Goravan, a couple of miles north of Heriz. Even professionals finds great difficulty in distinguishing between them. The Goravans, however, often sail under a false flag. They borrow patterns from the Heriz carpets, and call the result a Heriz-Goravan. However, neither the Goravan nor the Mehraban can compare with the Heriz.

As everywhere in Azerbaijan, the Turkish knot is used. The number of knots is low, and there is little variation in quality.

No. of knots per inch

	length	breadth	No. of knots per sq in
A	7	8	56
B	7	7	49
C	6	6	36

Meshed

MESHED or more properly Mashad — meaning Holy Place — is the Mecca of the Shiite Mohammedans. The eighth Imam Reza and Harun al Rashid are buried here. Its mosques and mausoleums are superb examples of Islamic architecture. A couple of centuries ago, Meshed was also Nadir Shah's capital. It was he who took the Peacock Throne as booty in New Delhi, and it was to him that Topkapi's famous dagger was to be presented. He was murdered, however, before receiving it.

Next to its temples, the town is proudest of its wool, which is in great demand also by weavers from other towns. "Peshm-i-Meshed" — the wool from Meshed — enhances the value of outside carpets. Local weaving, however, is in a period of decline, from which it seems unlikely to recover.

The town is in Khurasan, some 60 miles east of Teheran. Communications used to be slow and difficult, few buyers took the trouble to visit it. With no internal competition among buyers, prices were low. It was not worth the weavers' while to make better-class carpets when they were not well paid for them; and they could not get a good price for carpets of poor quality. Now that both wages and the cost of living have risen sharply, it does not pay to manufacture top qualities.

One often sees carpets with worn piles from the years between the wars, a lifetime that is no excuse for wear. This is due to the use of substandard material, excessively short-fibred wool. In the name of truthfulness, it should be added that an improvement has been made since the mid 50's.

The pattern earns very high marks. It is cultivated, tasteful, and with an elegant richness of detail. The ornamental designs used are decorative: flowers, palmettes, rosettes, arabesques, cloud ribbons, "Mir i botah" — all arranged with an artistic hand. The medallions are consistently attractive. The border, which on earlier carpets had numerous guard bands, now has only three, containing wave-like or chained garlands. The small prayer carpets of c. 5ft × 3ft 3in usually have both a prayer niche and Tree of Life in the field. Illustrative carpets are rare, but attractive inscriptions are to be found. The better carpets are often signed by their proud makers.

The dyes are almost always organic. There is plenty of madder in Khurasan, which gives a deep red color. The second main color is indigo. Bright carpets are very rare.

The most attractive pieces are to be found among the large carpets. Such carpets are donated to the mosques by rich pilgrims; the mosques are overfull of them, and the Mullahs sell a few about every other year.

The warp and weft are of cotton. Both Persian and Turkish knots. The carpets with Turkish knots are known as "Turkbaffs", and are usually of higher quality. This has nothing to do with the relative merits of the two methods as such, but because the Turkish tribe does not use the simplified "jufti" knot.

All possible measurements can be found, from 2ft × 2ft 8in up to 26 × 20ft.

The quality gradings are as follows:

	No. of knots per inch		
	length	breadth	No. of knots per sq in
A	17	14	238
B	13	11	143
C	11	10	110

Nain

NAIN is a small town near Isfahan, which manufactures exclusive carpets on an extremely small scale. Every carpet from Nain is among the most closely woven creations ever made by human hand. Extremely fine fabrics used to be made in the town, and the yarn-spinners became masters in producing the thinnest of yarn from the fine, very soft wool. No wonder that the number of knots on a Nain carpet *starts* at c. 400 per square inch!

Nain carpets are intended for persons with an eye to quality and a well-filled wallet — and such people abound in the Orient. Even if such carpets cost a lot, the price is never in fair proportion to the long, scrupulous work devoted to them. The many millions of knots contained in a single carpet also explain why so few products from the town are available.

In spite of their technical perfection, these carpets are somewhat uninteresting. Production dates back only a few decades, and the weavers have no old patterns or traditions to fall back on. Apart from a consistently light ground, the carpets lack any specific characteristics. Both the medallion patterns and those consisting of ornamentation over the entire surface are related to those found on the Isfahans. However, their perfection of execution seems to prevent them from acquiring a "personality" of their own.

The dyes, like the wool, are of the finest conceivable quality. The warp and weft threads are of cotton. The pile is cut very short. Persian knots.

The quality gradings are as follows:

No. of knots per inch

	length	breadth	No. of knots per sq in
A	23	21	483
B	20	19	380

Occasional carpets are to be found with over 650 knots per sq.in.

Sarab

SARAB is a fairly small town in Azerbaijan, between Tabriz and Ardebil. The name is associated with the town's speciality, its stiff, heavy and consistently light-colored Gallery carpets.

Their weight and stiffness are due to the thick warp and weft threads, and to their being very firmly knotted.

The pattern is closely related to several nomad designs: hexagons, rhombs or up-ended squares. The rest of the field — or only the corners — is usually filled with narrow oblique lines.

Previously, only Gallery carpets were on sale in the bazaars; then, in the 60's, carpets of c. 9ft 9in × 6ft 6in or even larger began to appear. This was a positive development, since the pattern came more into its own on a large surface than when compressed onto a slim Gallery carpet. Carpets with a wine-red or dark blue ground are also produced, and these have become extremely popular in places.

Sarab competes successfully with carpets in the same weight class and price range, such as Mehrabans and Goravans. Production is not on a large scale. So far, manufacture is still dominated by the Gallery carpet, a good utility product displaying no great artistic ambition.

The warp and weft are of cotton. Turkish knots. Little variation in quality.

The quality gradings are as follows:

No. of knots per inch

	length	breadth	No. of knots per sq in
A	9	10	90
B	8	9	72
C	7	8	56

Saruk

AROUND THE TURN of the century, the carpets of Saruk had a Kashan-like pattern with a medallion, and with the entire surface strewn with flowers, palmettes and spirals. These were of 6ft 6in × 4ft 3in or 5ft × 3ft 3in in size; they were thin, and had a light field with green leaves and a rusty red color that is otherwise common only in Malayers and Feraghans. These carpets are now extremely precious.

Today's Saruks are produced not only in Saruk but throughout the Arak district. They are strong, closely woven and extremely popular. They are known in Persia as "Saruk americani", since they were originally made to order for American importers. It was the latter who decided the pattern, the colors, quality and measurements. Even the height of the pile, which was fixed at a minimum of 0.4in.

The rusty red color vanished. It was replaced by old rose or bright red, both very popular in America and later also in Europe. The buyers also had their own ideas about the pattern, which often resulted in a highly decorative mixture of oriental and western ornamentation. Even today, it is mostly the same pattern that is manufactured: borders with garlands of flowers, and flowered medallions. The two entirely oriental patterns woven in addition are the garden pattern, in which the field is divided into panels containing different trees, flowers and "Mir i botah", and a rich ornamental pattern covering the entire carpet. This latter proved particularly successful, thanks to its calm, very harmonic surface.

Carpets are manufactured in all conceivable sizes from 2 × 4ft up to 17 × 26ft, or even larger if the customer wants a special measurement. Since these carpets weigh some 0.7 lb. per sq ft, a carpet of about 17 × 26ft weighs about 300 lb! In the past few years, the range of ground colors has been expanded to include azure or indigo, or turquoise, according to the vicissitudes of fashion.

The wool is extremely good, the carpet incredibly hard-wearing. Such rare carpets as are made of Merino wool are much more expensive, but they look and feel like velvet. The warp and weft are of thick cotton.

The quality gradings are as follows:

No. of knots per inch

	length	breadth	No. of knots per sq in
A	13	14	182
B	11	11	121
C	10	10	100

See plates overleaf

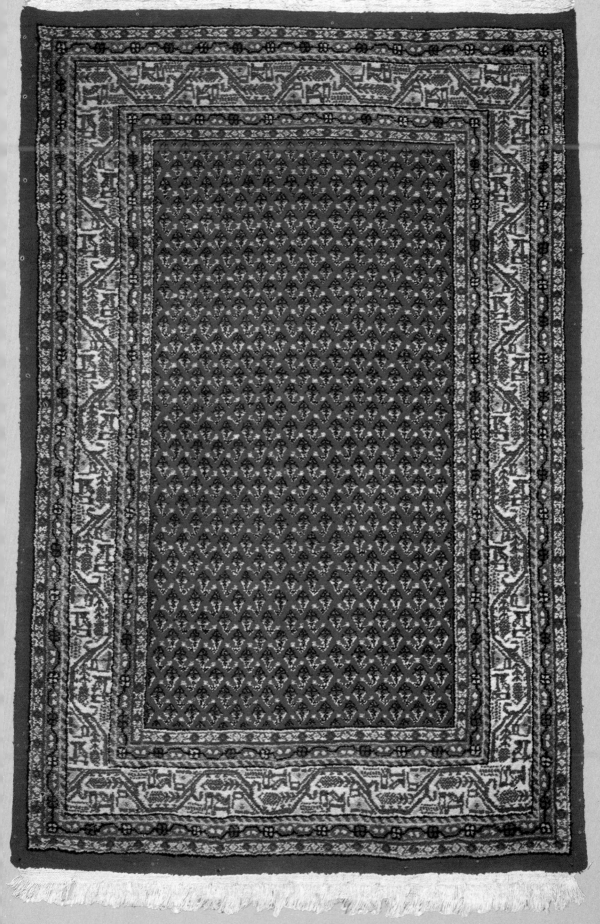

Semnan

SEMNAN is an ancient town, some 120 miles east of Teheran. It was of great importance during the age of caravans, since it was on the route of pilgrims to the holy city of Meshed. The day of the caravans, however, has passed, as has the town's former glory. Its only remaining object of pride is its thousand year old Friday Mosque.

And its carpets. These are the most Persian carpets imaginable. The pattern is curvilinear, flower motifs are mixed with pure ornamentation in perfect symmetry. The source of their inspiration was probably Khurasan, since the majority of them recall the old Meshed carpets with their rich ornamentation, particularly those with medallions. No monochrome surfaces, no symbols. Nor are any illustrative carpets made, this probably for religious reasons.

The wool, too, resembles that of Meshed, and it is quite possible that it comes from that district. The dyes are from vegetable substances, at least those used in all the older carpets. There is no organized production, and the number of carpets cut down from the looms is unfortunately very small. Warp and weft of cotton. Persian knots. Quality for the most part even.

No. of knots per inch

length	breadth	No. of knots per sq in
14	17	238

Sehna (Senneh)

THE LITTLE Kurdish town of Sehna lies 5500 ft above sea level, some miles from the Iraq frontier. Its name has a magic ring to the connoisseur, owing to the fantastic carpets produced there. These are among the thinnest and most magnificent ever created by human hand.

Thick, heavy carpets of a somewhat nomadic character are made in various places in Kurdistan. The carpets from Sehna are refined products, completely uninfluenced by those around them. Since the pile yarn, the warp and weft are extremely thin, the number of knots is very high — particularly if the cotton weft threads have been replaced by silk. Their manufacture takes a very long time. The population of the town is very small, and annual production thus very limited. It is estimated that a maximum of 70 small carpets are made per year. This explains why they are so rare, so much in demand, and so expensive.

The sheep of Kurdistan live at great heights, and have been endowed by nature with a strong, tough wool. Its fibres, however, lack the rich animal fat of the plains' sheep. The pile is sheared as short as possible, to some 0.14—0.16 inch. Since the pile sticks straight up, the light encounters the cut surface of the fibres in such a way that they cannot reflect. However, this lack of lustre is generously compensated by the pattern emerging with correspondingly greater clarity.

Variations in the pattern are only minor. Pink roses, "Mir i botah" and "Herati" motifs predominate. The two former usually cover the entire field, while the latter occupies for the most part only the medallion and four corners.

The dyes are usually the purest of vegetable dyes, seldom synthetic. Apart from a wonderful golden yellow produced from vine-leaves, sky blue and pink, the colors are of darker shade. The predominant color is indigo. Red occurs very infrequently, and then in a subdued tone.

Sizes are around 6ft 6in × 4ft 3in and 5ft × 3ft 3in. The larger carpets are of far earlier date, perhaps from around the turn of the century. That they are still in good condition is simply evidence of the unbelievable durability of these thin Sehna carpets.

The quality gradings are as follows:

No. of knots per inch

	length	breadth	No. of knots per sq in
A	11	13	143
B	9	13	117

Seraband

THE PROTOTYPE of these carpets is the "Mir". These were also woven in the Seraband district, south of Arak. No oriental carpet has been so frequently copied by western factories as this one. For centuries, the pattern has consisted of a single ornamental design: small "Mir i botah" close against each other, row after row of them from border to border. The border had up to 15 guard bands of different breadths, in different shades, and of varying decoration. The widest border always contained a coiling, leafy vine. The carpet was closely woven, and relatively short-cut.

Seraband carpets first appeared in the late 19th century, as a cheaper alternative to the Mir, but it was not long before they dominated the market. They were first sold as a cheaper Mir, but subsequently called simply Serabands. Their pattern is simpler; the "Mir i botah" no longer have the same chiselled appearance, and the number of guards has dropped to three.

Since there was always a demand for cheaper products, the Seraband gradually deteriorated. There is no point in listing all the grades, since carpets with yarn almost the thickness of string should not be let in the door. These were originally intended for low earners in the Arab countries themselves, but they found their way to the majority of European markets.

The Seraband often has by way of medallion a square turned through 45°, with two protruding arrows and sometimes brightly colored corners. The colors are synthetic, and their quality on a level with that of the carpet as a whole. The warp and weft threads of are cotton, the latter for some reason being dyed blue. The pile is cut fairly high. The ground is usually red or dark blue, with the higher qualities also beige.

While the old Mir was for the most part long, the Seraband occurs in all conceivable export sizes according to the potential market.

	No. of knots per inch		
	length	breadth	No. of knots per sq in
A	14	9	126
B	8	8	64
C	6	6	36

Shahsavan

DON'T LOOK for this name on the map, you won't find it. It is neither a town nor a village, but the name of a nomad tribe whose route extends from Ardebil down to south of Malayer. This is a long way, almost 270 miles.

Shahsavan means "faithful to the Shah" or "Protectors of the Shah". Abbas the Great ordered this warlike Turkish tribe to protect the area against the repeated attacks of the Osmans; these attacks, by the way, were the reason why the Shah left Kazvin and built up a new capital, Isfahan, at safe distance from the danger zone. This was around the year 1600, but the Shahsavans are still on patrol.

Their annual long travels left their mark on the tribe's carpets. It was impossible to avoid being influenced by all the carpets seen in villages passed over the course of almost four centuries. Many women married into the tribe over the years, and continued to weave in the same way and by the same patterns as they had learned in their native villages. As a result, many patterns were added whose origins can be traced to Aserbaijanian, Caucasian, Kurdish and Arak carpets.

Strangely enough, their ornamental designs never include the "Herati" or "Mir i botah", nor any spirals or curvilinear patterns. We find, on the other hand, barbed crosses, geometrically correct octagons, up-ended squares or rhombs, plus ornamentations and primitive animals in a fully patterned field without a medallion. Many carpets, however, have a very narrow red-white guard in the border which helps in identification — probably a tribal mark.

These carpets are highly original — and hard-wearing. The women of the tribe tend to spin the yarn themselves, and color it with vegetable dyes of their own making. The warp and weft threads can be either wool or cotton. The typically nomadic sizes are mainly 6 × 4ft, or long carpets, c. 9ft 3in × 4ft 3in or similar. No very large or very small carpets are woven. Production is decreasing every year. The Shahsavans prefer to sell their wool rather than make it into carpets, it is more profitable. Turkish knots.

The quality gradings are as follows:

No. of knots per inch

	length	breadth	No. of knots per sq in
A	8	8	64
B	7	7	49

Shiraz

SHIRAZ lies near the Persian Gulf, high up in an attractive valley. It is a town of roses, wine, poets, dervishes and philosophers. For centuries, people have made the pilgrimage to Shiraz to visit the tombs of Hafiz and Saadi. No one praised beauty like Hafiz, no one loved it more than Saadi, who actually believed that ugly people should be forbidden to visit the mosque, since they disturbed people's worship.

It is to Shiraz that the dozen or so nomad tribes of the Fars district drive their asses and camels to sell their carpets to the merchants in the bazaars. All these carpets — apart from those of the Kashghai and the Chamese federation — are termed Shiraz carpets. No carpets, however, are woven in the town itself. Some of these nomad tribes are artistically very gifted. Their naive figures and lively colors reflect a spontaneous joy in living.

Today's Shiraz carpets are among the thinnest in all Persia. The colors are dull, dark blue, dark red, dark grey and dark brown. Even the fringes are dark, being of goat-hair. The only bright color is provided by occasional bone-white knots.

The pattern is geometrical, mainly with medallions in the form of rhombs or up-ended squares. The field is usually filled with all kinds of symbols, amusing figures, stars, spear-heads, birds, animals, small Trees of Life and nameless ornaments.

The large amount of fat in the wool gives the dark colors life; the carpets have a lustre. Their becoming worn after only a few years is due not to the wool, but to the thinness of their weave. Their only positive property is their cheapness.

They are made predominantly in small sizes, which give the quickest money. 4ft × 2ft 9in, 5ft × 3ft 3in and 6ft × 4ft 6in are most common formats, since the tribesmen weave their carpets squatting in front of horizontal looms. Extra large or Gallery (runner) carpets are rare.

The "Mecca-Shiraz" belong to the Kashghai carpets; neither in their quality nor range of colors do they bear any resemblance to today's Shiraz carpets.

The warp and weft threads are mainly of home-spun goat-hair, so that the fringes are very dark. The manner of knotting is Persian, but "Turkbaffs", carpets knotted in the Turkish manner, do occur.

The quality gradings are as follows:

| | No. of knots per inch | | |
	length	breadth	No. of knots per sq in
A	12	12	144
B	8	9	72
C	6	8	48

Tabriz

THE CAPITAL of Azerbaijan lies in north-western Persia, some miles from the Russian and Turkish frontiers. Until the end of the caravan age, it was Persia's most important centre of trade and carpet-weaving. From Tabriz, the Western World was furnished with the Persian and Caucasian works of craftsmanship it so desired. The businessmen organized studios which made the finest-quality copies of old carpets. Many new patterns were also created. No other town can show anything like its all-round production. In the composition of medallion carpets, the main source of inspiration was the old hand-decorated book covers. The medallions were then divided into four, and placed in the four corners of the field. They are never so dominant as in, say, the Kermans, but are subordinated to the overall impression.

The thoroughly patterned surface, on which the pattern is repeated with mathematical symmetry, can bear not only palmettes, cypresses, weeping willows and arabesques, but purely Caucasian, geometrical ornamentation. With rhomb medallions, the "Herati" motif is also common.

The pictorial carpets of Tabriz are famous. The "four seasons" is an allegory of the life of the Azerbaijanian peasant. Other popular motifs include famous ruins of mosques and palaces, with which the district abounds, and the magnificent vases and bowls found by archeologists. And pleasant pastoral scenes. Most frequently portrayed, however, are the four great poets from the 11th to 13th centuries: Firdausi, Hafiz, Saadi and Omar al Khayyam. Countless other motifs are borrowed from reliefs in the ruins of Persepolis, such as the king's battle with the winged lions or the Old Persian King Djamshid sitting bolt upright on his royal throne, fanned with a palm-leaf by his slave.

The carpets of no other towns can rival the beauty and imagination of the borders on these Tabriz carpets, whether composed of garlands, trumpet-blowing angels, geometrical figures, or cartouches with inscriptions. These inscriptions are quotations not from the Koran, but from one of the immortal works of the poets. It is worth finding out the correct translation, and enjoying the beauty of their centuries-old verse.

There is no limit as regards size. The warp and weft are of cotton. Turkish knots.

Several of the town's studios still sign their carpets, i.e. knot their names into them. A signature, however, is no guarantee of quality, since it is no longer only the best carpets that are signed.

Carpets from before World War I are rare in the trade, and attract much higher prices than later products.

The quality gradings are as follows:

| | No. of knots per inch | | |
	length	breadth	No. of knots per sq in
A	18	20	360
B	15	17	255
C	14	14	196
D	12	13	156
E	10	9	90
F	7	8	56

116

Tafresh

TAFRESH is a small village 90 miles south-west of Teheran. It is situated between two great carpet centers, Arak and Hamadan. The carpets made in Tafresh often surpass in quality many better known and more expensive names.

The colors are in pastel, old rose with a touch of Cardinal red. They are not to be found on other Persian carpets, but more often on those from Samarkand.

Strangely enough, the pattern, which is to say the medallions on the only pattern they have, also has something Mongolian about it. In general, these carpets display a semi-nomadic character. This is reflected also in the disproportionate use of the light beige natural wool. The border is usually of this, and tends to upset slightly the attractive harmony of the pastel colors. Those carpets on which this hard, bright color does not occur are of greater value.

Their ornamental designs include one that is highly original: it looks like a knight from a set of chess pieces. These knights are usually placed in rows — horizontally or vertically — and can be found also in the border. They run like links in a chain.

The round medallion and four corner pieces seem to be village's only pattern. Only after World War II was a new one added: simply executed small birds on leafless trees, drawn with straight branches — a product intended for export, and one that in no way achieves the quality of the original Tafresh carpets.

It is mainly dozars that are made, c. 6ft 6in × 4ft 3in, but smaller sizes of the new pattern are to be found, e.g. 2ft 8in × 2ft, 4ft × 2ft 8in and 5ft × 3ft 3in.

Warp and weft of cotton. Turkish knots. The quality is fairly even:

No. of knots per inch

length	breadth	No. of knots per sq in
12	16	192

Tuisserkhan

TUISSERKHAN lies some ten miles south of Hamadan, in a romantic valley of the Alvand mountains. The entire district consists of four dozen villages at most. Carpets are woven in all of them, but carry the name of the district, not their own village. Since production was never on any large scale, they were usually shipped to the West in what are called "mixed bales" from Hamadan, in whose bazaars they were sold. The buyers simply called them Hamadans. Nowadays, the carpets proudly bear their own name — and justifiably since Tuisserkhan is a very fine product with a character all its own. Its most striking properties are:

1. The field is practically always delimited by a zigzag line along the border, whether it contains as medallion three upended squares or a single one with long spearheads. Or else the motif of the larger carpet depicted, which is one of the most interesting: the Tree of Life with three human beings as its fruits.

2. The main colors are indigo blue or beige. The red ground predominating in the neighbour district is never used.

Malayer, so famous for its carpets, lies not many miles from Tuisserkhan, and it would have been a miracle if the weavers had not been influenced by certain ornamental designs from their neighbour. The loan, however, is restricted to the border, which displays certain resemblances to the Malayer.

The wool is excellent, as are the dyes. Since the yarn has a good lustre, the indigo can shimmer in all the varying shades of night. Warp and weft of cotton. Turkish knots.

The quality gradings are as follows:

No. of knots per inch

	length	breadth	No. of knots per sq in
A	9	8	72
B	9	6	54

Veramin

VERAMIN is a small town less than 40 miles east of Teheran, with a small-scale production of high-quality carpets.

These carpets are easy to recognize. The pattern consists of "Mina Khani" ornamentation: large, round, simply drawn flowers, row after row of them, linked together by diagonally running stalks. No medallions or corners, no flourishes on the stalks.

The dominant color is indigo blue, with a trace of violet. Two other colors which are effectively used are orange (very sparingly) and the grey beige natural wool.

These carpets are thin, the pile is short-cut, and they are of outstanding quality. They are not, strangely enough, popular in Persia, in spite of their good qualities. The Persians call them "mushammad", linoleum. In their eyes, the "Mina Khani" pattern is profaned by this likeness to a chequered bathroom floor. Fortunately, the people of Veramin stick to their traditions. These fully patterned carpets fit into any environment, old or new.

They are made mostly in two sizes: the dozar, c. 6ft 6in × 4ft, and 9ft 9in × 6ft 6in.

The wool is excellent. Warp and weft of cotton. Persian knots. The colors are improved if the carpet is chemically cleaned by a professional. They become softer.

The quality gradings are as follows:

No. of knots per inch

	length	breadth	No. of knots per sq in
A	10	13	130
B	8	12	96

Yezd

YEZD is an ancient town. Alexander the Great used it as a prison, and Marco Polo praised its silk brocades. Its clay buildings with their rounded cupolas lie buried in the earth to protect them from the heat, and the air is conditioned by minaret-like wind drums. Yezd is the spiritual centre of the relics of Persia's Zoroastrians, the few who defied Islam's demand that they convert. They do not bury their dead, since the earth exists to bear harvests, not to be polluted by corpses. Nor do they cremate them, since fire is for them the symbol of absolute purity. Instead, there exists in Yezd a Tower of Silence, whither the dead are carried and left to the vultures.

The art of carpet-weaving never flourished there in the old days. As non-Moslems they had no need of prayer carpets, nor of overdimensioned carpets for the mosques. The few carpets woven were for their own homes.

Manufacture with an eye to export was started only at the turn of the century. They had, at that time, only two patterns: the "Herati" and a medallion carpet with a rythmic repetition of flower and tile motifs. Today these carpets are rarities, but they attracted no appreciation at the time. Success was not achieved until artists and weavers from nearby Kirman were called in. The new product was confusingly like the flowered Kirmans. The same sort of woollen yarn was used, and the same blueish red color made from cochineal.

Laymen found it difficult to distinguish between the two. Nowadays, it is easier. The red of the Kirmans has become livelier, while the Yezd has kept to the old shade. The obverse side of a Yezd is brownish in tone, since the weft threads are brick red; those in a Kirman are beige, light blue, or the same color as the front.

The Yezd always attracted a lower price than the Kirman, although it often surpassed the original. You seldom saw a Yezd with "jufti" knots, i.e. a knot looped over four warp threads instead of two, something which is more frequent among the Kirmans. In recent years, however, the Yezd has also deteriorated.

Sizes are mostly around the medium. It is rare to find a carpet of less than c. 7ft 3in × 4ft 3in or more than c. 9ft 9in × 6ft 6in.

Warp and weft of cotton. Turkish knots.

The quality gradings are as follows:

No. of knots per inch

	length	breadth	No. of knots per sq in
A	14	15	210
B	11	12	132
C	9	10	90

Zendjan

ZENDJAN is a little town in Kurdistan, just over 100 miles north-east of Bijar. Until the mid 60's, the carpets from this town and the villages around it were well-known but nameless. They lay stacked in high piles in the bazaars, mixed with the products of Qulyahi, Senjab, Koltukh, Songhor, Gurani and other Kurdish tribes and villages, and were sold under the name "Kurdistani".

As the manufacture of carpets ceased in many villages, and several tribes found it more advantageous to sell the wool than weave it, Zendjan pulled into the lead as a supplier of carpets. It furnished the markets with what they wanted: carpets of commercial quality, at reasonable prices.

These carpets are made of the tough but lustreless wool of Kurdistan. The pattern is geometrical, and drawn with astonishing correctness. There is a wealth of variation, but then the weavers of Zendjan cheerfully copy the special patterns of other Kurdish and Aserbaijanian villages.

The dyes are almost 100 percent synthetic. The blue colors resemble the famous sky blue of the old Sehna and Bijar carpets, they are seldom as deep as indigo. The red dyes tend to have an admixture of orange. The latter also occurs unblended, but it is well balanced and not a real source of irritation.

Warp and weft of cotton. Turkish knots. The number of knots is fairly low, because the "jufti" is used, i.e. each knot is looped around four warp threads instead of two. In spite of this, the carpets seem closely knotted and they are fairly hard-wearing.

There is little variation in quality. You can compare with the standard quality given below:

No. of knots per inch

length	breadth	No. of knots per sq in
7	7	49

126

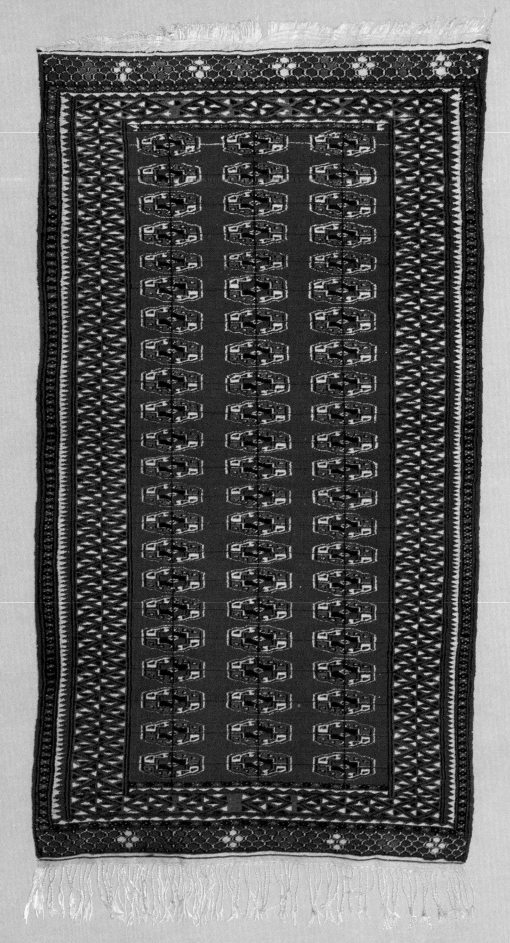

The Pakistani Carpets

THE CARPETS we must expect to see most of in the future are from Pakistan. Manufacture began shortly after the partition of India, when the new state of Pakistan was founded.

Outstanding carpet-weavers have been living for centuries in Amritsar and Shahjahanpur, men whose ancestors knotted the priceless Indi-Isfahan carpets for the palace of the Grand Moguls, and for the great mosques. When Amritsar was assigned to India, the Moslem carpet-weavers were moved over to the nearby Punjab, the most attractive part of West Pakistan.

In spite of the great economic difficulties they faced, the weavers succeeded in acquiring some small looms and set to work at once. It was impossible to hold out for any length of time without revenues. They therefore restricted themselves to prayer carpets, about 6 × 4ft in size. Such a carpet could be finished in a few months. To step the tempo up still further, they used only the Bukhara pattern which they knew backwards, and were aware was popular in many places. They dared not even dream of making large carpets of 13ft × 9ft 9in, such a project might have taken four people a year and a half to complete. Unfortunately, they used the cheapest yarn available in the bazaars. The state sold off every year the army's used socks, from which the buyers spun new yarn. The short-fibred waste yarn had no strength in it, and the carpets became worn after only six to eight months.

The businessmen from Europe had angry complaints from their customers, and balked at the idea of further purchases. Such carpets were sold only by auction firms, which avoided responsibility by displaying them in advance.

Meanwhile, Pakistan's balance of trade deteriorated. To stimulate exports, the government promised exporters a high bonus. In the case of carpets, the bonus was no less than 40 percent.

This was an entirely different proposition. Wealthy businessmen set up dozens of looms, bought yarn, and employed masters with their own teams consisting of three or four small boys between the ages of five and ten, who received a weekly wage. They reckoned that the high bonus would permit them to sell the carpets below cost price, and still make good money on them.

More and more businessmen adopted the idea, and production was soon in full swing. The moment was a favorable one. The Shah of Persia's program of industrialization was taking many people from the looms to better paid jobs, and the prohibition of child labor was strictly observed. Persian carpets became much more expensive.

The smart Pakistani businessmen avoided repeating the weavers' mistake of using cheap yarn. They bought the best local and imported worsted, spun from the wool of Merino lambs. This wool is very rich in animal fat, and gives a unique lustre to the carpets. The Bukhara pattern was retained, but sizes increased. Carpets were made from 2ft 8in × 2ft up to 13ft × 9ft 9in, or even larger to order.

Since the yarn was machine-spun and of even thickness, the manufacturers could guarantee deliveries of even quality. The warp was carefully counted while it was set up on the looms. Countless random samples revealed that the number of knots per square inch was practically identical, regardless of what team made the carpets.

In the beginning, even these better carpets encountered tough resistance. Their evenness

A Bukhara carpet manufactured in Pakistan. These are often seen in the shops with the designation Pak-Bukhara or P. Bukhara.

had its disadvantages: these carpets were far too perfect. They lacked the small unevennesses of their Persian cousins: the sides that were not always straight, the small deviations in color shades, the improvisations of pattern — all the charming and desirable details that guarantee a carpet as hand-made. The merchants, however, fell for the low price, and the new experiment was more successful.

To acquire a wider range, the Pakistanis began to copy the Persian carpets. They took patterns not only from carpets and the professional literature, but from the catalogues of European department stores showing machine-made carpets with oriental patterns! The latter was a somewhat unhappy source of inspiration.

The new carpets were bastards. The Pakistani scale of colors differs essentially from the Persian. Nor do they reproduce the character of the Persian carpets, since the same woollen yarn is used in all patterns, and the makers forget to cut the pile higher or lower as in the different Persian districts.

The same applies to the imitation of Caucasian carpets. The Pakistanis can never produce a "genuine Caucasian", the yarn of which is hand-spun and uneven, and in which double or triple weft threads are used according to local tradition. The Pakistani Caucasians look as if they were machine-made, although they are not.

The Pakistanis dismiss such details as unimportant. They claim that at most 10 percent of people who buy carpets are connoisseurs, the rest simply want to cover their floors with "genuine, hand-made oriental" carpets — and this is what they offer. They count on the ignorance of the customer — and they are unfortunately right.

To see a carpet studio in operation is an experience. You enter a vast courtyard, some 45 × 45 yards in area, totally blinded by the burning sun over your head. Around the courtyard runs a concrete roof about 4 yards wide, which throws a merciful shadow. A mysterious intoning is heard on all sides. Only when you enter under the roof do you see the long rows of looms, set up about one yard apart and manned with one team each. The intoning is from the masters who sing out the colors, and the oldest boys who repeat them. Some 150 masters and 500 boys work simultaneously. At a high tempo, and with vast concentration. As soon as a carpet is completed, it is cut from the loom and a new warp set up so that work can proceed without any great loss of time. One or more carpets are completed every day.

When the pile has been sheared as evenly as possible, the washing of the carpet commences. This is an even greater experience. Eight men work in a mechanical rythm on each carpet of about 6 × 4ft.

The carpet is placed on a stone floor, in the open air. Two men each pour a bucket of water over the carpet, from a tank. Two others run over the length of the carpet, brushing away the water with heavy fibre brushes. Four men then press further water out of the carpet with a sort of iron scraper. The same procedure is repeated at least twenty times. And they are not gentle about it, neither with the brush nor the scraper! You stand there in silent amazement, wondering how long the carpet can take this sort of treatment. But it seems to stand anything, and when dry it is a perfect, durable carpet that can be tramped by human feet for decades without becomning worn.

The washing masters can also treat carpets with chemicals, if they want to tone down excessively vivid colors or give them a selling finish. The great bulk of carpets, however, are simply washed with a great deal of clean water, and even more labor.

It is easy to grade the qualities, since the Pakistanis sell them according to exact classifications such as 11/18 or 12/20 etc. These figures mean that the carpet has 11 or 12 knots per inch lengthwise, and 18 or 20 across. To arrive at the number of knots per sq in for the 12/20 quality, multiply the figures 12 × 20 = 240 knots per sq in.

The current gradings are as follows:

A	12 × 24 per inch	= 288 knots per			sq in
B	12 × 20 ” ”	= 240 ”	”	”	
C	11 × 18 ” ”	= 198 ”	”	”	
D	10 × 18 ” ”	= 180 ”	”	”	

For knots tied in the Persian manner:

A	16 × 18 per inch	= 288 knots per		sq in	
B	14 × 16 ” ”	= 224 ”	”	”	
C	13 × 15 ” ”	= 195 ”	”	”	
D	9 × 12 ” ”	= 108 ”	”	”	

Pakistani carpet with Caucasian pattern.

Index

Numbers in italic refer to pages
where illustrations may be found